D1530259

#BEMORE

77 Secrets
to a Better Life

By: Sandi Krakowski

Copyright © 2014 by Sandi Krakowski

All rights reserved. No part of this publication may be reproduced, distributed, or transmitted in any form or
by any means, including photocopying, recording, or other electronic or mechanical methods, without the prior
written permission of the publisher, except in the case of brief quotations embodied in critical reviews and certain
other noncommercial uses permitted by copyright law. For permission requests, write to the publisher at the
address below.

Scripture quotations, unless otherwise noted are taken from The ESV® Bible (The Holy Bible, English Standard
Version®) copyright © 2001 by Crossway, a publishing ministry of Good News Publishers. ESV® Text Edition:
2011. The ESV® text has been reproduced in cooperation with and by permission of Good News Publishers.
Unauthorized reproduction of this publication is prohibited. All rights reserved.

ISBN 978-0-9894934-3-7

eISBN 978-0-9894934-9-9

Fedd Books
Post Office Box 341973
Austin, TX 78734
www.thefeddagency.com

Published in association with the literary agency of The Fedd Agency, Inc.

Editorial services by Cara Highsmith, Highsmith Creative Services, www.highsmithcreative.com
Cover and interior design by Mitchell Shea

Printed in the United States of America

First Edition 2014

CONTENTS

Introduction

Part I: Be More . . . Connected to God   1

Part II: Be More . . . In Tune with Yourself   39

Part III: Be More . . . Attentive to Your Relationships   87

Part IV: Be More . . . Engaged with Your Community   125

Part V: Be More . . . Mindful of Your World   155

About the Author   187

INTRODUCTION

When I first started posting on Facebook and Twitter, my only purpose was for business. My approach? The typical business approach of mentioning my products, talking about what I did, and hoping someone would buy in.

We were at 10,000 followers on Facebook and about 5,000 on Twitter when something crazy happened. I was in Maui, Hawaii and God was talking to me in the early morning hours when this thought came to my heart: What if you spend your time on social media encouraging, empowering, and equipping? I remember my mind racing through the typical thoughts of: *What does this look like? How do I do this? Will it help my business? What is my purpose?*

I didn't have all the answers and, to be honest, now that we have more than 1 million people connecting on our social media pages, having those answers really isn't important to me anymore. But I do know this: people are changing, lives are healing, and we're making a difference.

Our sales quadrupled in a year; we've created more jobs; and, living in a fish bowl hasn't been as hard as I thought it would be. A fish bowl—you know, on display for all to see. That thought nearly paralyzed me. I'm not perfect. I get cranky. The only thing I know to be is real. When I tried so hard for years to do, do, do, do, do, I got lost and didn't even know me.

But through this process I've learned how to BE MORE. This is what I'm all about. This is what this book is all about—BEING—the concept of being more. We have thousands of stories that have poured in of people who are thinking differently and dreaming again. Multibillion-dollar brands are seeking out my marketing help. But the core of it all—the main purpose of my mission—is to turn the lights back on in people's hearts and minds and to see a generation of Champions arise who know how to BE MORE.

This book is your manual for a better life. Being more starts with looking up to strengthen your relationship with God and then ripples outward. Think of this as a series of moments with you and God together, and you are taking into the world what you receive.

The book is broken into five parts that focus on the different areas of our lives where we encounter disappointments, frustrations, and setbacks. When one is out of balance, others begin to suffer. If we aren't listening to God, the negative messages that flood our minds distract us from what we know is true. When we place too much value on what others have, we become dissatisfied with our own gifts and blessings.

As you go through this journey, you are going to discover how to BE MORE connected to God, to BE MORE in tune with yourself, to BE MORE attentive to your relationships, to BE MORE engaged with your community, and to BE MORE mindful of your world.

BE MORE is designed to be carried with you so you can read a section when you are in need of direction or inspiration. Each secret closes with a Tweetable phrase so you can share inspiration with others. Put this book on your coffee table. Hide it in your purse. When you set on this path to BE MORE, you can live an incredible life, even in the challenges, even in the small simple things. I GUARANTEE YOU . . . you will have a better life and it is EASIER than you think!

With love,
Sandi Krakowski

BE MORE . . .
CONNECTED TO GOD

PRAY! ASK! THEN GIVE
GOD TIME TO
ANSWER.

BE MORE . . .
CONNECTED TO GOD

Our journey to *being more* starts with being more connected to God. There is one very simple reason for this: He designed us for a life of greatness, and the quest to be more is about stepping into that greatness. It is imperative we understand that our connection to God is what helps us discover that purpose, stay focused on progressing toward it, and fully become who we are supposed to be.

The secrets in this section address the many obstacles we encounter that keep us from trusting God and make us doubt ourselves and His plan for our lives. These issues include lack of self-esteem, fear, the need to control everything, and the inability to love ourselves enough to accept His goodness and His blessings.

As you read through this section, think about where your relationship with God stands right now. *Do you believe He created you for something special or do you doubt He cares enough about you to make an effort? Do you trust that He will answer your prayers and be there for you or do you wonder if He is even real?*

I pray you will find answers to the questions that keep you from living fully in His rich blessings and that you will find the comfort and security of knowing He is there to guide you each step of the way. I pray you will grow closer to Him in this journey and step into the greatness He has planned for you.

This BE MORE movement is all about claiming God's purpose for your life and letting that take you beyond where you are now. You are on an incredible journey, and I am excited to see where it takes you and how it helps you grow.

GOD IS TAKING SOME OF
YOU ON A NEW PATH.
TRUST HIM!

SECRET #1
YOU CAN TRUST GOD IN ALL THINGS

I don't know what you're facing today but this one thing I do know: God hasn't changed.

He still shuts the lion's mouth. He still parts seas. The problem with this generation is that often we're so complacent and comfortable that we believe a miracle is when God prevents bad things from happening and makes our lives easy!

And when we don't get the big, flashy miracles, we think God has abandoned us. We have this tendency to think the glory of a loving, powerful God is best demonstrated when we walk right into a fire and He extinguishes the flames. But the truth is, He is greater when the fire surrounds us and He prevents us from being consumed!

Easy isn't always better.

Just as fire purifies and refines metal, when we go through trials, we are being made stronger and more fit for our purpose. It is okay to take a risk and believe Him for something so big that you'll look like an idiot if He doesn't show up!

God is a strategist and He knows how to deliver us. He still opens deaf ears. He is still in the business of resurrecting dead things. He can still call to the four winds and blow fresh air onto your impossible situations!

I still believe that He is sufficient and that there is *nothing* you will ever face that He cannot help you press through. Stir up the gift that is in you! Lift the hands that are weary!

I remember when all three of my boys were sick with the flu and I stayed up all night with them. I was exhausted and wondered if I would ever make it through. As I lay with Justin in my lap, Bobby on the couch next to me, and Jeremy in the other room, I began to pray. God assured me that I would survive this, reminding me that I could sleep that night because He never does. He is constantly watching over us and seeing to our needs. He reminded me that I can always trust Him, no matter the trial.

When the storms of life come, rest upon the rock who knows your name. Take comfort in knowing He has your back. He will not let you fall because He created you to BE MORE.

Believe in the little things. Stop waiting for someone to walk on water to ignite your faith.
#BEMORE

SECRET #2
CATCH GOD'S VISION FOR YOUR LIFE

We declare prophesies over our lives every single day with our words and our prayers. God declares prophesies over our lives as well.

He says, "You are seated in heavenly places!"
He says, "Nothing will be impossible for you!"
He says, "I will never leave you!"
He says, "To the one who drinks of me I will give Living water!"

Do you know God sees you into your future and you're getting better every day? Catch that vision and cling to it! You have a remarkable gift in God's plan for your life. And, you can either make the choice to align with it or to fight against it.

When we allow other voices to interfere with what God is telling us, we can get off track. Whose voice are you listening to today? Are they voices that contradict what God wants to give you?

One of the most empowering moments in my life was when I discovered I had a switch in my mind that I could flip to turn the negative chatter into positive messages. Unfortunately, we will never be able to stop the negative noise from getting into our minds. As long as we are human and alive, we will be under assault from the enemy, whether he is using our critics or our internal voices to distract us. But, we can control how much we let that affect us and how long we let it go on.

You can tune out the negative chatter. Don't give permission to anyone who is trying to influence your thoughts or your life in a way that distracts you from the prophecies God has declared over your life. Your future holds great promise, and if you shut out the negativity and focus on where you are supposed to go, you will see those promises fulfilled.

In your future, you are stronger. You are doing better. Catch up! It's waiting for you. God has a great vision for your life and has promised to give you great blessings. He wants you to join Him.

He wants you to see all the potential you hold and claim it. He wants you to BE MORE.

Your life is a message someone is reading every day.
Give a bold message of God's great love and the
greatness we are designed for!
#BEMORE

SECRET #3
ASK GOD FOR HELP

God wants to be the first place we turn when we need help. He wants to be the "go-to" guy for all of our needs. Pray to Him and ask for help with everything—help with your family, your work, your play—I mean *everything*.

You can be the biggest pest heaven has ever seen. You are allowed to be the kind of person who asks God for so much help that when you get to heaven the angels breathe a sigh of relief. Do you know why? Because in asking God to guide your steps, meet your needs, and fill your heart you are showing Him how strong your faith is.

It is essential in all of your asking that you believe. I mean *really* believe. Get your hopes up so high it borders on absurd. It's good for your heart and your soul to test how much you can trust God. Ask, Ask, Ask! And then ask some more.

Learning to ask God for help was not easy for me. I am a very independent woman and was really used to taking care of business on my own, dealing with struggles my own way, and finding my own answers. When I finally realized this wasn't working as well as I thought it was, I knew it was time to make a change.

Knowing myself, I had to start small. I asked God for help in getting over a headache. I asked God to help me get a good parking space. I relinquished control over little things until I could get used to the fact that I wasn't in charge. Over time, I was able to turn more over to him and start asking for help in the work I do or for help in knowing what to say in the boardroom. I also learned I can trust him with the really big things in life. (Of course, I am still asking for His help with the good parking spots, too.)

God is overjoyed when he gets to answer our prayers. He is pleased to shoulder the burdens and cares we cast upon Him. When He gets to bless us, He is equally blessed.

God is not growing tired of you. He is not simply tolerating you. He is celebrating you. Join Him in His efforts to help you BE MORE.

When we are humble enough to ask for help, we'll go places. Ask God to help you today. Have faith that He will. EXPECT IT!
#BEMORE

SECRET #4
GOD LIKES YOU!

Your thought for today: God not only loves you, He likes you.

He doesn't look at us as sinful, disgusting people, but as tender children He loves and adores. After all, He sent Jesus to give us all we need and to fix our mess. He's not mad at us! He is for us, not against us. He delights to give good gifts.

Yes, He has feelings and is hurt very deeply when we ignore Him. His greatest desire is to see us live in favor, grace, peace, and power. It is important to him that we know how much He cares about every single thing, every detail of our lives.

He created us with all the love he has in Him and though we may disappoint him, it's not about getting angry. He just wants the best for us, and when we take our eyes off of Him, we make it difficult for Him to lead us to the abundance He has set aside for us.

I truly believe that one of our deepest needs is not only to be loved but also to be liked. The reality of our relationships is that we can absolutely love someone while not really liking them. You see, loving someone is a deep and abiding thing that allows us to have care and concern for their well-being. It is what keeps us connected. But, liking someone means that even with their flaws we enjoy spending time with them. We seek out their company and find our interactions with them rewarding and enriching.

It is possible to love your sibling who has brought pain to the family and dislike their behavior and life choices. In those cases, we don't really get enjoyment out of spending time with them. On the flip side, we can like the coworker we have lunch with every day or our college roommate who is a lot of fun without ever developing feelings of love toward them.

When we get to like the person we love, it creates a whole other dimension to the relationship. The things you do together mean more because you like and love one another. The great news is that God doesn't just love you because he loves all of His creation unconditionally. He really and truly likes you, too. He went to great effort to create someone very special and you mean a lot to Him.

Stop listening to those who do not teach the true nature of God and who are controlling, scaring, and threatening people into submission. This is a tactic of the enemy to keep us from fulfilling our purpose. Keeping us afraid of God prevents us from seeking Him and His guidance for our lives.

The enemy knows that with one glimpse of the deep, deep love of God all the darkness begins to disappear. It's absolutely amazing what happens when one human being realizes they are loved by God and He's not mad at them.

When you know this truth, no matter what happens in your life, you can take comfort in the knowledge that God is on your side. My friends, this is the key to BE MORE.

Live in harmony with God's delight for you and resist the enemy's accusations. Our authority grows in the Father's delight!
#BEMORE

SECRET #5
GOD MADE YOU GREAT!

Anyone who ever became great in history had a vision of the greatness God had placed in them! This is not about arrogance or ego.

Actually, arrogance and ego do not have a vision for the greatness God gave them because they overcompensate and attempt to be something they are not! Those who cling to a false sense of value not rooted in who God made them to be are in constant struggle to feel worthy.

When we are not attuned to the greatness God placed in us, we constantly feel the need to prove ourselves. We experience a serious lack of belief in who we are, and that stands in the way of doing great things. Those with genuine power and humility see the greatness God created in them and steward the heavy responsibility of that greatness. It is very humbling and, at times, even a burden.

So how do we get great? Lean into God.

Inside each of us is a little kid dreaming of greatness—the astronaut who will go to Mars, the firefighter who will run into a burning building to rescue people, the princesses who will save their kingdoms, and the superheroes who will fix the world. This isn't just a childhood fantasy. I believe we dream of greatness because God made us to be great. He gave us the DNA to be something really special.

Let Him make you and mold you. Believe in who He says you are and allow Him to position you where you can live out the greatness He intended for you. Trust God to lead you to the plans He has that will cultivate and support your greatness.

When you become more, you empower others to do

the same. It's not about you or me. It's about us. It is about playing your part in the perfect plan God has and contributing to the greatness that He intends for everyone because it all works together for good.

Believe in your greatness! God put it there! God intends for you to BE MORE!

The critical pieces of life are stacked and lined up together. It's important that YOU be you and focus on playing your part!
#BEMORE

SECRET #6
EXPECT MORE . . . BE MORE

How many times have you asked yourself, *What if it does work out?*

Seriously, what if all those dreams you've had actually start to come true and things start going your way?

One of our biggest barriers to success is our tendency to prepare for failure. We try to protect ourselves from disappointment and to avoid expecting too much out of life.

Do you realize what an insult that is to God? When we try to calculate how He is going to do what He said He can do, we are not really believing in Him. In fact, we are making Him smaller.

But when we believe God for bigger and better, it is insulting to the enemy. When we couldn't care less about how He does what He said He will do and just focus on doing our part, it gives God all the room He needs to blow our expectations out of the water!

The power of expectation is incredible. Don't worry! I'm not taking you down some metaphysical, new-agey, path. Expectation is something God wove into our very being. The power of expectation is a gift from God. It is hope, the promise, the faith He asked us to place in Him.

Expectation is a double-edged sword. For the person who is always expecting failure and always expecting loss, they will find exactly that. The person who is always expecting things will come together and is always expecting favor will see those blessings in their life.

Think about it: Children do not expect that Santa Claus will disappoint them (until some cantankerous adult who is stricken with skepticism starts to shoot down their dreams!) No! They lay out cookies! They believe!

As we grow older we are almost groomed to doubt, to be skeptical. We become conditioned to think this is the way to protect ourselves so we will never be disappointed. We know the pain of disappointment and come to believe it is better to just suffer, to live in constant lack, and to struggle than to ever allow ourselves to hope that something might work out. We rely only on what we know we can do for ourselves.

But deep inside of us, placed there by God, is a spirit of hope. It is a reminder of God's promises—a knowing, a longing to expect more . . . to BE MORE.

When we are full of doubt we attract reasons to support this belief. Then our brains go to work seeking failure. Change that.
#BEMORE

SECRET #7
GOD IS NOT MAD AT YOU

Sometimes we grow weary. We've worked hard, done all we can, and feel we are spinning our wheels. A wicked spirit comes in these moments to make us think God is mad at us. We hear lies in our heads like:

He's angry and you are going to lose everything.
You are foolish and look like an idiot.
You're not good enough and God is upset with you.

We begin thinking that if taking a step forward—stepping out into our dreams, paying our tithes when we are struggling to survive, or going the extra mile—that we will be disappointed and God will let us down.

My friends, I stand in the gap right now in the name of Jesus Christ and declare that God is not mad at you and that you are enough!

When these thoughts come, we need to repent for thinking He'd ever let us down, let us go, or abandon us. He is a loving God who cares about us and endures through all of life with us. This is when we should stop and be thankful. Remember the blessings you have, the ways He has shown up in a big way, and the times He has carried you through struggles.

We are not promised a picture-perfect life, but we are promised that if we believe in Him we will never go through it alone. We must lay aside our doubts and fears. We must ask for forgiveness and be thankful. His heart is wide open to us. He is a good God. He is KIND. He does not reward faithfulness with lack or kindness with meanness.

Go openly and honestly to your Heavenly Father and let Him know you are trusting Him again and you are sorry for your unbelief. Share with Him your fears and concerns, and he will comfort you and fill you with the courage and the peace to keep going and to BE MORE.

We all face trials and challenges in life. We also have reasons to thank God, to be encouraged, and to be hopeful! Focus there!
#BEMORE

SECRET #8
RECEIVE HIS LOVE

How well do you know Jesus? Is He just that man you learned about in Sunday School and accepted into your heart as a child? Or as a teen at a retreat? Is He alive and real in your life? Are you fully connected to the relationship you can have with Him?

Let's get to know Jesus a little better. He is slow to anger and always forgiving. He is kind and full of compassion. His mercy is enduring and His grace is abundant. He is sufficient to meet all of our needs. His love heals ancient wounds of bitterness, overcomes all hatred, does not condemn, offers peace for our pain, and is truly life-giving. His love for us burns deeply, abides eternally, and saves us fully. Jesus loves. Jesus paid the price. Jesus died. Jesus is enough.

When Alan and I were still newlyweds, we had one of those blow-the-roof-off arguments where frustrations were just more than we could take. We knew we loved each other, but our communication had completely broken down. I fell to the floor beside my bed and cried out to God, rehashing the argument, word-for-word. In a moment of clarity, I said, "I am so glad you know all of this. I need you to help me love Alan the way you love Alan."

I was consumed with peace then as the comforting knowledge settled over me that He really does know all that is going on. He still loves all of us in spite of the stuff and nonsense we try to hide from him. If we can learn how to see ourselves and others the way He sees us, and receive that love He has for us, we will be able to love just as deeply and unconditionally.

Receive Him. Receive His love. It's simple. Just say, "Jesus, I receive your forgiveness for my sins. I receive your kindness for all of my unkindness. I receive your compassion for all of my hate. I receive your healing for all of my bitterness. I receive your peace that casts out all of my fears. I receive your perfect love for my life."

Knowing Jesus more personally allows us to know more of who we are and who He wants us to be. Connect with Jesus and BE MORE.

Be consistently and constantly confident in who God says you are AND who He says He is! Not occasionally. Consistently!
#BEMORE

SECRET #9
SHUT OUT THE DEVIL'S CHATTER

The greatest trick the devil is pulling off in our lives today is convincing us that we don't matter and that God is no longer relevant. Stop being vulnerable to the devil. If we were more impressed with God than we are the other things of the world, the devil would have no power.

In this day of technological advances and media saturation it is very easy to forget these simple facts:

- God parted a sea so more than 3 million people could pass to the other side on dry ground and not be destroyed by their enemies.
- A blind man was able to see after Jesus coated his eyes with mud He made from his spit and dirt on the ground.
- The children of Israel were able to win the battle of Jericho by walking around the city and praising God.
- The Prophet Ezekiel spoke to a valley of dry bones and they came to life.

Okay, this last one really trips me out! *Lord of the Rings* has nothing on God. God told Ezekiel to breathe on the bones. Then marrow in their bones began to grow. Flesh began to form. Hearts began to beat again. They came alive. Not just a few, an entire army!

We forget who our God is and how great He is when the devil comes and brings his doubt and fear.

He whispers,

"Who do you think you are?"

"What makes you think you can do this?"

"How are you going to overcome all of these obstacles?"

"Why do you think anyone is interested in what you have to say?"

And we allow him to get in our heads and distract us from what we are called to do when our response should be:

"Oh, I know exactly who I am and whose I am, and so do you. That's why you taunt me."

"Well, I know I can't do this on my own, but I can do all things through Christ who strengthens me."

"If God has called me to this, He will make a way."

"I don't know for sure, but this one thing I do know, you lying spirit: I do not want to listen to you! Now be gone in Jesus name!"

Stop being so susceptible to his taunts. Don't let him play in your mind. Trust the awesome power of God's hand on those who believe in Him. Shutting out the devil's chatter and tuning in to God's promises will allow you to BE MORE.

You are in a war! There will be those who argue with you, fight your dream, mock your passion, and seek to stop you. Rise up!
#BEMORE

SECRET #10
DON'T LET 'EM GET YOU DOWN

Don't be so hard on yourself. Give yourself and others grace. Become your own best friend instead of your own worst enemy.

We tend to be unnecessarily critical of ourselves and that gets us down and makes us insecure about ourselves. Insecurity breeds self-hatred, and self-hatred causes us to turn on those around us.

I've learned how to identify this in myself because I've been there before. When I notice that I am being hard on myself and everyone around me, I know God has some tending to do and I need His touch. In the deepest part of my struggle I was shut off—closed heart, massive pain, horrific trauma, and all messed up. I was shattered. I was growing cold, and I didn't want affection from others. In fact, all I wanted was more space—as much space as I could get—between me and those in my life, between me and the rest of the world.

But Jesus came and fixed me. He healed my wounds, relieved my pain, and restored all the broken pieces from the trauma. It was a process. I had to learn not to be so hard on myself and to give myself grace—kindness, gentleness—something that, oddly, can be harder to give ourselves than others. I had to understand that I was worthy of that. You are worthy of that too.

Mistakes happen. We all fall. We all do things that we later wish we could change, take back, or redo. That's okay. Just stop being so hard on yourself. Make a habit of taking good notes. Learn from your experiences. Every lesson is a stepping-stone on the path to greatness. Every weakness is an opportunity for growth. It's not easy and can be very painful; but, it's always, always worth it.

God knows how to fix us. He knows how to love us. If you ask Him to open your heart wide, He will show you how to BE MORE.

Keep getting back up. That's the secret of successful people. We all make mistakes. We all get weary. Get back up!
#BEMORE

SECRET #11
STOP WISHING UPON A STAR

Wishing—wishful thinking—this is not faith. In fact, it's a cousin of doubt. Wishful thinking is throwing a request out into space, hoping God is sitting out there ready to catch it and maybe toss a blessing back at you. It's like throwing a penny into the wishing well and hoping the distant gods of the world will somehow, in some magical way, answer you.

Wishful thinking isn't intimate; it's distant, and I'm not even sure it is hopeful. It is haphazard and careless, and this is not the character and heart of the God of the Universe. That is not how God operates. He is not distant; He's personal. He never said, "Come to me and wish that one day I will answer you." No, He said, "Seek me with your whole heart and, if you do, you will find me."

Too often we hold back from fully believing. We hedge our bets by treating it casually or by not getting our hopes up. But God wants us to be confident in him and go after His blessings with abandon.

Think of it this way: Do you remember how when you were a kid you would jump from one piece of furniture to the next? Maybe you were hopping from island to island like Godzilla. Or you'd line up the kitchen chairs all in a row like they were the tops of skyscrapers and you were a superhero bounding through the air from building to building. You were confident and fearless. You didn't close your eyes and hope you'd make the next leap. You didn't cross your fingers and wish that you'd land. You just believed it would happen.

Even though this was a child's fantasy, it is a good illustration of the kind of faith without reservation we must have. We need to believe that God will be there to receive us if we make the leap. God is longing to have a relationship with you. You don't have to wish He will bless you; you have to believe He will. Trust God to help you BE MORE.

Believing IS receiving! You can't receive until you believe! Hoping is not believing! Have confidence that believes BEFORE it sees!
#BEMORE

SECRET #12
WORDS HAVE GREAT POWER

It starts with a seed. A single thought.

Before we know it, this thought has taken root and we begin to believe it; we buy into it. Soon this thought has consumed our hearts and our minds. It takes over and begins a process of destruction and despair. These words that start the cycle can come from others or they can be messages we tell ourselves.

I remember my own struggles with this. I still recall the excruciatingly painful words spoken over me—the kind that make your knees cave and your heart sink. I remember accepting those words into my mind, then watching them grow from seeds of self-doubt into a complete absence of hope. Eventually, I collapsed and lost all desire for life.

Then . . .

A new thought.

A new seed.

A new root.

As His light appeared through the shadows, I could feel Him again. Jesus walked into the room and said, "You are going to make it through this and will tell millions of people."

In my broken state, I replied, "I can't even talk to myself without pain in my heart. How on earth will I ever talk to millions of people?"

He simply told me, "You will. Trust me."

Trust is difficult, especially when you are trusting for a complete reversal of the situation you are in and of the mindset you have. It is a cycle. We repeat what we focus on. We plant seeds every day. We are gardeners, you and

I. And guess what?

We can refuse to allow some seeds to take root! We can take out our tools and say, "I reject that! I don't receive that!" Being the master gardeners that we are, we can choose, with an act of our free will, to NOT let those thoughts take root in our lives.

Words have great power, and just as the single negative thought brought you down, this single positive thought— *Jesus is with me!*—will lift you up out of the darkness and give life to a new way of thinking and speaking.

Speak His truth. Plant the seed and tell yourself you are ready to BE MORE.

Refuse to allow negative thoughts to control you. PUT a smile on your face. CHOOSE the tone of your day. DECIDE to trust God.
#BEMORE

SECRET #13
TAME YOUR TENSION

Do you feel tension creeping up on you? Are your muscles tightening up? Is your jaw clenched? Pay very careful attention to that tension. Many times that is a signal that you are right in the middle of God's will with the best thing that could ever happen to you right in front of you. The enemy of your soul, your future, your finances, and your life will create tension when he sees that you are on the verge of working in God's plan.

The enemy will make you feel like quitting; you'll begin to have feelings you've never had before! The tension will begin to invade your sleep and even your home! When you are pursuing your dreams, the enemy does everything he can to disrupt your path. You'll begin to buy into the lie that, if this is right, it should be easier. He will tell you that struggle shouldn't be a part of your life if you are on the path God wants for you. Tension is one of the great deceivers and discouragers.

Remember, when you are on target, you become a target. The devil does not want you to stay where you are in God's will and will try to get you off track by convincing you the rough road is not the right one. You will not create the life of your dreams without some tension. You will not push against the status quo without some resistance.

When I decided to go in a new direction with my career path, I encountered so much tension I began to question my choices. I had people challenge the wisdom of my plan. I received advice that I should try something different since this was so difficult. I began to wonder if I had made the wrong decision. This is when you have to dig in. This is when you have to pray to God for discernment and declare what God said instead of what your feelings say. God has grace equal to the tension, so stop running, stop stressing, and lean into heaven. Heaven holds your answer: "I can do all things through Christ who strengthens me."

Ask heaven to shut the door on the lies and deceit. Stand. Stand. Stand. Keep standing and you will see the glory of the Lord. You will see Him leading you out of the tension to the promises He holds for you. Don't let tension define your path. Let God show you the way through the struggle to BE MORE.

No matter how difficult, you can rise above your challenges. Don't lose sight of your future.
#BEMORE

SECRET #14
GOD LIKES TO THROW CURVEBALLS

God is never short on surprises. In fact, He loves to sur-prise us. He will be working on something and I am be-lieving and praying. He gives me pictures and visions and dreams, and then, way out of nowhere, He throws a curve ball I never expected! Everything changes instantly. The landscape changes. The atmosphere shifts. The map is rewritten. It's a whole new dimension—a new level in a flash!

Have you ever been through one of those fierce storms when the sky goes dark, the wind howls and bends the trees to the ground, and the clouds swirl and turn almost green from the atmospheric turmoil? It can be terrifying how the lightning rips through the sky and the thunder shakes you to your bones. And then, all of a sudden, it stops. The sun pierces through the darkness in beams that I like to call curveballs from heaven.

And in these moments I can hear God laugh. Have you ever heard God laugh? He sure does. I sit there at times thinking I'm gonna predict His every move. I am His daughter you know; I've got Him figured out . . . or so I think. God loves to have a playful, loving relationship with us. I think He sits in heaven strategizing how to throw a wrinkle in our plans.

At times I wonder if He's impatiently jumping up and down, shouting, "OH COME ON! WILL YOU PLEASE BE-LIEVE ME? I have something to send your way, but I can't do that until you trust me!"

So often, the enemy throws a stupid, small something or other that sends us reeling, panicking that our plans are derailed. And God is up there thinking, "WHAT? You have no clue what I have in store for you! Get back up my sweet daughter! He's bluffing you! Call his bluff! Trust ME!"

We wobble. We weep. And we stand back up. Scared . . . no, terrified. And then God gives us that curveball that makes everything even better than the plans we put together that the enemy unraveled. God's plans for us are so much better anyway, so trust Him. He knows just how to help us BE MORE.

God is a strategist and will position you exactly where He wants you! It can feel like the wrong place or the wrong time. Defy odds. Trust Him!
#BEMORE

SECRET #15
YOU HAVE PERMISSION TO ENJOY LIFE!

How many of us are not enjoying our lives or living our lives to the absolute fullest? When we can look past our circumstances, our worries, and our fears, what is left? A life that is there for you to live and enjoy!

You have full permission to enjoy life even as you are growing, even in the midst of struggle. There is no special place where everyone else is experiencing their great life because God just waved his hand and whisked them away to this magical place. Everyone has to grow, some of us more than others, and every phase of life has good and bad in it.

I had to grow in many ways in many areas of my life. There were so many layers to peel through at times I thought I would die—literally die. But even in all my dysfunction and learning to be more of who God made me to be, I was speaking to stadiums of people who needed a life line.

My heart would see those faces, and I'd think, *How the heck can I help anyone else when my own life is such a mess? Surely God has made a mistake. Yes, I believe the Bible is true and I know that it says God doesn't make mistakes, but maybe He was being too optimistic with me and what I was really capable of accomplishing.* Of course, I was wrong about this and He was right, but it took me believing there was room for me to help others while I was healing.

As you are working with God on changing your life, don't beat yourself up when you blow it. Forgive yourself and keep going. Don't get discouraged; don't give in; and don't quit! Enjoy your life even while you're getting whole. Enjoy your life even while you're learning to be more and be free.

Learning to live differently, think differently, and walk with the Holy Spirit through every area of life is a journey and it takes time. It's perfectly okay for you to be happy, to forgive yourself, and to take one day at a time while you are in the process of learning to live your best life. After all, if you are wallowing in doubt, frustration, and disappointment, how in the world can you work out the rough stuff and break through to the good God has planned? Be kind to yourself. Forgive yourself. BE MORE.

Decide that you will live a wonderful life. Everyone has problems, but we can choose joy and find peace in God right now!
#BEMORE

SECRET #16
THE ME GOD MADE ME TO BE

The trap of performance-based acceptance is a prison very difficult to break free from once you're caught in it. The lie of performance is deadly, and the scariest part is that it can have the appearance of being polished and perfect. Some of the most put-together professionals are actually children who are walking around in an adult life, still living in that cage of seeking approval.

Most of my past is laced with pain, shame, and feeling I didn't fit in anywhere. As far back as I can remember, I felt out of place. Preschool, grade school—all levels of school were very painful, trying to find acceptance. I bet there are a lot of you reading right now who can relate.

I dreamed of entering modeling school as a young woman. But this passion was the pathway to discovering anorexia. I had no clue one could survive on such small amounts of food. Having observed my mother battle with food, depression, and her weight my entire life, I was sure you would fall over dead if you attempted to live on small amounts of food. When I learned you could actually get very thin on less than 500 calories per day and that most major modeling schools encouraged this, a world of starvation was opened to me.

This eating disorder would follow me through life. I wasn't set free until about five years ago when God completely delivered me from my obsession with the size of my hips and waist. But I encounter the residue of such pain every single day through the hundreds of thousands of people I meet on social media—people obsessed with being someone other than who God created them to be.

I remember the first time I realized God had called

me to write, speak, and share my story. There were two voices in my head: one was confident and the other worried what people would think.

But when I came to understand the truth of how God sees me, it drew me even closer to the path of BEING more, not DOING more.

Who I am = What *Jesus* did + What *God* thinks of me
Who I am NOT = What *I* can do + What *others* think of me

It is time for you to be free. It is time to lay aside the words of your personal demons, the opinions of others, and the pressure of society. There's only one thing we have to be, and that is who God made us to be—and God made us to BE MORE!

Your best life happens when you are walking in who God says you are and refusing to let your past ruin your future!
#BEMORE

WHATEVER YOU ARE
FACING, ALWAYS
REMEMBER YOU ARE
MORE THAN YOU THINK
YOU ARE.

BE MORE . . .

IN TUNE WITH
YOURSELF

DECLARE "I AM BLESSED.
I AM TALENTED."
ALL THINGS ARE COMING
MY WAY AND WORKING
TOGETHER FOR MY
GOOD.

BE MORE . . .
IN TUNE WITH YOURSELF

Being more in tune with yourself is essential for discovering where you are in this journey and where you need to go to reach your potential.

There are a number of terms and phrases you will see repeated throughout this book—purpose, potential, God's calling, greatness, champion, and BE MORE, to name a few. These all relate to your understanding of who you are and who you were created to be.

When we are not attuned to what is going on in our hearts and minds, we cannot truly understand what this journey is about, and we are far less likely to realize our full potential. The following section includes secrets that will help you learn how to be more in tune with yourself, addressing issues such as listening to instinct, building self-confidence, shutting out distraction, rejecting negativity, and taking time for self-care.

While we are often taught growing up that being selfish is bad and going the extra mile is the ideal, we tend to take these to extremes and end up neglecting ourselves. This is not about becoming self-absorbed and childish. This is about being self-aware and understanding your purpose in life. If we don't get that, we can't be all we are supposed to be for everyone else.

Real change starts on an individual level. The impact God intends for us to have on the world will never happen as long as we are stuck in cycles of negative, self-defeating thoughts and insecurity about our direction in life.

I pray you will find in this section the inspiration to really work on yourself and find the steps necessary to be more. I pray you will experience real growth so you can step into the greatness God designed you for. Take this time to discover something new and exciting about yourself and claim a life that is enriching to you and those around you.

BE REAL. PEOPLE WILL RESPECT THAT!

SECRET #17
KNOW YOURSELF

When I take personality and leadership tests, there are two traits that keep showing up: assertive and adaptive. This means I can lead and I can adjust.

Being assertive obviously is a strength for leaders, but being able to adapt to circumstances that are constantly changing is really beneficial as well. Being flexible saves you time, helps you go further, and gives you courage to try new things. It's your bounce-back factor!

But if you change your principles or the core of who you are so much that you find yourself being someone you're not, that's *not* a good thing.

Chameleons can change their color and even the pattern on their skin. They camouflage themselves to blend in. Have you looked in the mirror and discovered that you don't know who you are because you have "adapted" too much to your environment?

One of the best things I can tell you to do for yourself is to truly know who you are and what kind of people you want around you. I can't tell you how many times I have had people give me advice on who *they* thought I should be and who *they* thought I should hang out with. This is no good. You have to know yourself and what you really need.

Looking in the mirror—I mean *really* looking—can be both painful and revolutionary. It brings awareness. We spend so much time trying to meet everyone else's expectations and demands that, before we know it, the person looking back at us is someone we not only don't know, but someone we don't like.

Adjusting a plan or an approach is a good practice as

long as you aren't compromising your fundamental beliefs in the process. The only way to avoid this is to really get to know yourself. Know who you are, what you believe, why you believe it, and where you draw the line. Don't be afraid to stand up, stand out, and BE MORE.

You are not a chameleon. Being adaptive is great.
Losing who you are so that you blend in isn't.
#BEMORE

SECRET #18
TAP INTO YOUR INSTINCT

Recently our vet found a tiny kitten at a garbage dump. She weighed only half a pound and was very sickly. But she had a will to live. I saw this little girl sitting in a cage when I took my schnauzer, Kobe, in for a checkup, and that was the end of it. I had to have her.

I texted my husband and sons to inform them I was bringing a kitten home! Their replies were almost identical: "NOW? Like here? Like now?" It was fun walking in the door with the three-week-old kitten. Everyone immediately fell in love with her.

We did have to get one of those "playpen" type tents to keep her safe until everyone could get acclimated. Kobe wanted to treat her like a toy and Latte, our five-year-old Ragdoll cat liked to kick her out of the tent.

My sons had wanted a little pig for a pet, but that wasn't going to happen in my house, so apparently their retaliation against my decision was to name our kitten Chanchita, or "little pig" in Spanish.

Chanchita is doing great now. She is full of energy, and I've noticed she likes to stalk one of her toys—looking away as if she's disinterested and then pouncing on it like the mighty predator she's designed to be. I watch her and think, *Who taught you to act like a cat? How on earth did you learn to do that?*

Instinct is a powerful thing. We teach it to the business owners I coach. Instinct is your hard wiring, and being able to tap into that is essential for understanding your purpose and how to fulfill it. You were created with a unique design and a specific calling. A lot of people never discover their calling because they don't learn how to listen to their instinct.

It happens when you let yourself be still and hear what God is whispering to your heart. Figure out what gives you the most joy. What is that thing that makes you feel connected? What makes you feel you are where you are supposed to be? Doing what comes naturally—speaking, writing, performing, helping, healing—that is instinct and that is where you will meet up with God's purpose for your life. Look for ways to tap into your instinct because fulfilling that design and calling is a gift to the world! Instinct is your key to BE MORE.

No one else is like you. God made you specifically and strategically unique. This is your responsibility: to shine bright!
#BEMORE

SECRET #19
PURSUE YOUR PURPOSE

I meet people every day who are seeking their passion, but many are chasing a fantasy and don't realize it is not where they should be focusing their efforts. They seem to dislike hard work and think wealth just follows those who pursue their passion. But that is rarely the case. In fact, the only way that passions become productive are when they are matched with real effort. Passion + Work = Purpose.

Pursuing your purpose isn't a fantasy! Those of you who want to seek your passion may read this and think it makes life too serious and tedious, but pursuing your purpose can be fun. It can be exhilarating . . . and it can be the most terrifying and exhausting thing you've ever done! You see, what happens when you pursue purpose instead of passion is you are going against the stream. You will likely find yourself on a different path than the one 98% of the population is walking. To work hard, follow through, stay humble, be teachable, obey God, and serve others is not easy and goes against what we are conditioned by society to do.

We get consumed with the idea that chasing our dreams is going to somehow miraculously pay off with fame and fortune. The problem is we see a few rare individuals who took a chance, got discovered, won the lottery, or stumbled onto a once-in-a-lifetime opportunity and made it big. We cling to the fantasy that this can happen to us. And maybe it could. But, in most cases, if your passion is going to grow into a billion dollar enterprise, you are going to need to work hard, ask for help, and make sacrifices so you can live a life most people never will!

It's okay to have passions and dreams. They are important to innovation. But the only way they become more than fantasy is by digging in, rolling up your sleeves, and doing the work to make them happen.

You were made for greatness! Don't let the wish for it to be easy keep you from your purpose. Find your purpose and BE MORE.

To love our lives, we must be willing to make changes. Sometimes it's hard, but it's so worth it. Be more. Do the work!
#BEMORE

SECRET #20
FIND YOUR RHYTHM

Why do we try to push against our natural bent? Why do we try to force ourselves into things that are uncomfortable or incompatible with our nature? Learning to listen to your body and your natural rhythms is important for success.

For example, my energy is at full speed early in the morning. This is when I am most alert and functioning at my optimal level, so it would be silly for me to try to write my book, articles, or do other work that requires my best later in the day. I have learned it is a much better use of my time when I go with my natural rhythm.

Of course, that doesn't mean I get to lock myself into a cave the rest of the day and only do things when my energy is at its best. We don't get to just shut down and be selective about when we engage in our lives. But it does mean that when I need to meet with someone who is very important, or have a project that must get done, it is wise to pay attention to my natural rhythm and maximize that part of the day.

Maybe we've spent too much time pushing and pushing through long hours and days that are jam-packed and over-scheduled and have forgotten we had a choice. We fight against an invisible force we believe is holding us back, and we end up burning ourselves out trying to do what doesn't come naturally because, deep inside, we believe we don't have a choice.

We fight wars against ourselves and press ourselves beyond reason just to survive. We force ourselves into routines that aren't productive and actually end up wasting precious time when we would accomplish so much more if we listened for what our natural rhythm is and flowed with it.

Use your time wisely. You do have a choice, and you are the only one with the power to hold you back. This could be the year your dream comes true. Make each decision in alignment with that goal. Find your rhythm and BE MORE.

The secret to success in life: STOP doing things that war against your soul, and start doing more things that make you strong!
#BEMORE

SECRET #21
TAKE TIME TO TAKE TIME

When was the last time you took time to rest, time to feel, time to open your heart so you can sense God all around you?

Life is filled with obligations and stresses, lists and chores, and it's so easy to forget to take care of *you*, and you fail to let God Himself tend to your heart. You don't necessarily need a week off; you might just need to give yourself a few minutes each day so you can find your *WHY* again in the midst of worrying about all the *HOW*.

In the middle of your calling, your ministry, your business, and your purpose, don't forget to take the time to take time. Put your To Do list aside. Eat a meal a little bit slower. Put your feet up and rest awhile. Grab a blanket and lie down.

You have to remember this one critical thing: YOU ARE IMPORTANT. You matter, and you need to take care of yourself.

God has so many incredible things He wants to pour into your life, and He wants to use you to bless others. You can't be those things if you are weak and run down or distracted and discouraged. You are loved no matter what you're going through. God has not and never will change His mind about you. He knows who you are, why you were made, and the things He has planned for you.

Even if you make mistakes, if things fall apart, or if you find yourself caught between two rocks and four hard places, you will never be alone. Taking time to allow God to nurture your heart and restore you is essential for bouncing back from the difficulties and disappointments in life. It is what will allow you to do more and reach more people. A time of restoration and healing is what empowers you to fulfill that greater purpose.

Give yourself the gift of self-care. It isn't selfish or self-absorbed to make sure your own needs are met. I mean, let's be honest; who else is going to look after you, especially if you are the caregiver and nurturer in your family?

So, take time . . . to take time. Take time to BE MORE.

Keep your priorities right and be here for the long haul.
Say no when you need to and take action daily!
#BEMORE

SECRET #22
KEEP YOUR PERSPECTIVE

Many of the things we worry about are so big in our heads and then so, so tiny in reality.

A camera lens on a smartphone can take a very small object and make it larger than life. It can capture moments and turn them into an entire event. Mirrors provide a reflection and, depending on the type of mirror, what we see is altered. Some mirrors make things very wide! Some make things very tall and stretched out. Others shrink things into short, squatty reflections. We call them "fun house" mirrors at amusement parks.

These are all distortions of perspective. Something has altered reality to make it appear different. These distortions can be entertaining, but when we gauge the truth, make decisions, and calculate relationships based on a skewed perspective, we are operating without our hearts and heads in alignment.

Time management specialists tell us to write things down, map things out, and look at how we spend our time in small pieces. By doing this, we can get a better view of how things really are.

Have you ever had something on your To Do list that you absolutely despise—cleaning the toilet, sweeping the garage, purging the closets—because it never gets done? Over and over and over you think about it, prepare for it, and dread it. Before you know it, your perspective is completely out of whack! In your head it becomes an all-morning task! Yet, if you were to set a timer and get to work, it might, at tops, take 10-15 minutes!

The real problem is how much time we waste thinking about what we have to do, not the thing that needs doing.

Work on reframing your view of the things that trouble you. Instead of thinking about how much you don't want to do something, think about how great it will feel to have it done.

Take a deep breath. Process it on paper or with a friend. Put things in their proper perspective to BE MORE.

Goliath was not part of Gods plan! It was David's assignment to destroy him! Don't make your devil bigger than God. Slay that beast!
#BEMORE

SECRET #23
KEEP THE BIG PICTURE IN FOCUS

Are you bogged down in the details? Are things overwhelming you? Take a step back and refocus. Look at what you are trying to accomplish—the goal you are aiming for. Stop worrying about how you plan to get there and take a moment to remember why you are trying to get there in the first place.

When an architect sets out to design a structure, he doesn't start with the plumbing, electricity, or the paint color for the walls; he begins with the vision for the project. Focusing on details before we have the big picture in mind will drain our creativity and our energy.

This doesn't mean the details aren't important too, but if you don't know what you are building toward, it is hard to be sure you are laying the right foundation. The same is true in how we build our lives. If we don't know who we are designed to be, we can't be sure we are on the right path.

When you begin to "whelm" past your "over" mark, it's time to step back and take another look at the direction you are heading and be sure it is where you are supposed to go. Allow yourself to Rest. Pause. Just Be.

When the pieces and the bits don't fit and you're stuck in the details like a fly on sticky paper, don't get upset, just retreat for awhile.

It is my personal belief that if we took time to pause more through life, our doing would expand and we'd get more done in less time. If we are putting too much effort into details that don't really matter—steps that don't really lead us to our goal—we are wasting precious time and effort.

So, while you are making your To Do lists and checking off tasks, make sure this is really where you need to spend your time. Make sure these details actually work together in the composition of your big picture. Step back to see more and BE MORE.

Choose your battles wisely! No one changes the world by turning their attention to every problem they encounter! Don't be distracted!
#BEMORE

SECRET #24
PAY ATTENTION

Where is your attention right now? Are you thinking about what you have to do in a few minutes? Or maybe you're thinking about what is on your schedule for this moment!

It is really easy to get distracted from what we really need to be doing. For example, I am writing this book, but I need to go feed my dog, Kobe, and give him his shot and be able to come back here without getting unfocused. It won't be easy because as soon as I go into the kitchen, it will probably make me think I am hungry. And if I get hungry, I will need to make something to eat. And if I stop to make something to eat, I will most likely forget what I was writing about and my flow will be broken.

But Kobe is diabetic and needs his shot at specific times to live, and I have to take care of him. That means I have to practice discipline and self-control to be able to meet all of my responsibilities. I have to stay focused to make sure everything gets done.

When I forget or get distracted, beating myself up about it does not help, but getting back on track instantly does. Making a habit of paying attention to what I'm paying attention to has changed my entire life. God seems to have given me five brains that all think at the same time. It is easy for them to derail my progress, so it is critical that I direct their thoughts.

You may feel the same way. Being able to multi-task is a necessity for the busy and driven person, but successfully managing so many thoughts, interests, and demands also requires your focused attention. You won't do anything well if you are trying to do one thing while distracted by another. Multi-tasking is a delicate balancing act that can become a disaster if you aren't tuned in to what you are doing in each moment.

So, what are you thinking about right now? Are you fluttering from one task to another without seeing it through? Are you forgetting why you walked into a room, putting your car keys in the refrigerator, or driving to the office when you meant to go the grocery store? All of these are signs of distraction. Get focused, make lists, take some time for rest—whatever you need so you can be more effective.

Pay attention so you can do more and BE MORE.

To take back control of your time. It's important to guard where your attention is going. Learn what to ignore and what to tune in to.
#BEMORE

SECRET #25
GET OUT OF YOUR OWN WAY

I have spent more than three quarters of my life getting in my own way. I had one excuse after another for why I couldn't be all God intends for me to be—the trauma I experienced, the people who have held me back, and the obstacles that were in my way.

One day I realized it was all a conspiracy going on within me. My "lesser" self was strategizing against my greater self, seeking to stop me. Some might call it my weakness, others my sin nature. I don't think it's either of these. I think it was the part of me that was terrified of the champion I would become if I got out of my own way. It was the part of me that knew there would be no more room for excuses if I stepped into my greatness.

It was then that I decided to fight for my destiny, fight for my future, and throw open the doors of mediocrity and smallness I'd been hiding behind for so many years. I chose to throw the doors open and just shine.

Shining isn't always easy. Some people hate it when you turn the lights on because they've been comfortable in the darkness for so long they don't want to see what is revealed by the light. But, I've encountered more who are grateful—those who have been looking for the light switch for a long time.

When I turned the lights on in my own life, I gave others a little light to find their way too. By removing my own barriers, I began to open the door to their freedom as well. Stop making excuses. Stop finding reasons to avoid what God has planned for you. Get out of your own way and BE MORE.

Be serious about running the race that is set before you. Come hell, high water, ups or downs, make a choice to live a great life!
#BEMORE

SECRET #26
RETRAIN YOUR BRAIN

What are the negative messages you tell yourself? Do you find your brain running along a track of self-defeat? You can retrain your brain.

It starts with reinforcing a new way of thinking—redirecting your brain to different, more positive thoughts. It may sound like I'm oversimplifying this, but it really does come down to a choice. Make the decision today that you're going to learn to live differently.

Tell your brain, "Today I'm going to start believing EVERYTHING God has said about me!" Say it out loud, "I don't have to listen to my critical, negative inner voice anymore! I was created in the image of a Holy, Kind, Loving GOD!"

If these negative and critical voices start talking, just grab hold of those thoughts and make them obey you. "Thought, I don't have to listen to you."

Taking control and telling them they don't have power will release you from being a prisoner to your thoughts. We have to do the work of a champion to live the life of a champion.

One of the first computers I ever had was one of those big towers that sat under the desk. It was a dinosaur, and I really had no idea how it worked. My sons added games to it and I tried to use it to run my small business. Eventually, it stopped working and nothing worked to fix it. Finally, a computer technician told me I needed to override everything and basically wipe the hard drive clean.

Sometimes our brains get so bogged down in wrong thinking that we need to do an override to reset them. This is when we have to take command of our thoughts and make them support our goals—make them open up our futures.

When you have a hard day and the thoughts overtake you, don't beat yourself up, just get back up. All warriors have hard days. Some have to retreat for a while. But the truest nature of a powerful warrior is to GET BACK UP, and the only way to do that is by refusing to listen to the negative messages in your brain. Retrain your brain to believe in you. Retrain your brain to believe you can BE MORE.

When we start making the right choices, it feels good. The good feelings will silence the negative voices in our head when we keep going!
#BEMORE

SECRET #27
DON'T CONCERN YOURSELF WITH THE OPINONS OF OTHERS

When we believe one way, yet act in another, we're existing in a state of conflict. We're also in a state of DIS-EASE. We are disconnected and paying a heavy price for that.

Trying to be someone you're not is a heavy burden. When we are more concerned with everyone's expectations than we are about being who God designed us to be, our beliefs end up in direct contrast with our abilities and potential. Maybe you went to college to get a degree simply because everyone told you it's the only way to make money. What if you joined the family business because it was expected from the time you were born? Even worse, perhaps you have stayed in a relationship because you don't want to hurt the other person's feelings.

These are significant life choices and too many of us make them to please someone else instead of doing what we know is right for us. When we let the desires of another have too much influence over the choices we make, we are disconnected from our own lives.

Everyone has an opinion about something. Ironically, people seem to have more opinions about what you are doing with your life than they do about what is going on in their own. There are only two opinions that really matter: (1) the one you have of yourself and (2) the one God has of you. Everything else is really irrelevant.

Now, I realize that is really easy to say and not so easy to remember, especially when we care about someone and want them to value us. The key is to consider their opinion but not to value it over your own or God's. You have to align what you believe with your behavior. Focus on who you are designed to be, celebrate who you are, and trust that God made you exactly as He wants you because He knows what your future holds.

There is value in considering the opinions and advice offered by those who love you and want the best for you; but, at the end of the day, it is your life and your choice. Choose to align yourself with God. Choose to do what you feel is right for you. Choose to BE MORE.

Stop trying to impress people! Just be yourself!
#BEMORE

SECRET #28
KEEP ON PUSHIN'

The two things I have been hearing God say over and over are: (1) Punch fear in the face, and (2) Do hard things!

Fear is not a bad thing in and of itself. We are wired with fear to protect us from danger. But when it is the compass for our lives and becomes toxic it is no longer useful. Fear actually becomes more harmful than the danger we are alerted to.

When you feel fear taking control, punch it in the face, kick it in the teeth, slap it, and tell it to shut up. Tell this fear that God gave you discernment to know what you really need to worry about and shut down the rest of it. Then go on with your day.

It's that simple. Say, "Shut up fear," and move on. Part of putting fear in its place is learning to do hard things. You have to push yourself beyond your comfort zone. You have to confront things about yourself that are unpleasant. You may have to do a little "bigger belief body building" so you have the muscles to do it.

In my years of body building in the gym I discovered you have to learn how not to be afraid of the push. It is important to continually build on your routine, adding more weight, more reps, and improving your form. The same is true with our lives. In order to get to our goals and reach our destinies we have to know when to push. This can be uncomfortable, but it is so worth it. Once it becomes a lifestyle, doing hard stuff doesn't feel so difficult. It feels pretty normal.

Every time we try to push ourselves to a new level, we will encounter fear. If we want to accomplish big things and have a life beyond our dreams, one of the hardest things we will face is the fear that we don't deserve better or that every thing we are trying to build will come crashing down around us. Break free from that fear and do hard things so you can BE MORE.

Do hard things! In order to create the kind of freedom you desire for your future, you will have to do hard things now. Don't give up!
#BEMORE

SECRET #29
MAKE IT A HABIT

Whether you are trying to adopt a new attitude, break a bad habit, or start a new routine, you are going to run into that "lesser you" that has been operating a certain way for many years! They will fight back. They will resist change.

But it's going to be okay. Just keep doing it. Repeat it. Do whatever you can to find motivation. Keep reminding yourself of your goal and why it is important to you.

Did you know the word *enthusiasm* comes from the root word *entheos?* This means to be "in God."

When you are enthusiastic, you are in God.

Want to break bad habits and attitudes? Get enthusiastic about something GOOD!

Remember when you were young and you got a new toy and it became your focus? What about when you were a little older and decided you wanted to play a sport or learn a musical instrument and you devoted hours to it? Think about when you first fell in love and how consumed you were with getting to know everything about that person.

With most things in our youth, interests fade, enthusiasm wanes, and we move on to the next thing. Don't let your pursuits as an adult suffer the same short attention span. To make a lasting change you need to find that same powerful enthusiasm you had when you were young, but figure out how to maintain it even when the newness and the novelty wears off.

They say it takes three weeks to make or break a habit. Three weeks to the freedom of a new mindset or freedom from a destructive habit. Scientists tell us that repeating something seven times makes our brain begin to change. Anytime you try to start something new, the first four days are the most difficult. Oh my goodness they are difficult!

Use your natural enthusiasm about this new way of life to propel you forward and keep up the momentum through the retraining period. Tell that "lesser" you they won't win. Tell them you are changing and you will BE MORE!

No one has more control over your life than you do! Never forget that. Lean into God, rise up, and live your life!
#BEMORE

SECRET #30
YOUR STATE OF BEING PRECEDES YOUR STATE OF DOING

Are you one of those people who is constantly doing and doing but find yourself feeling unfulfilled, lonely, and confused? Maybe that is because you are too focused on doing and have forgotten how to be and *who you be*. No, I didn't just forget my grammar. I meant to say that. Long before we do, *we be.*

I talk a lot about purpose and who we are designed to be. It is important that we discover this and embrace our paths—to have a dream and pursue that dream. But don't confuse your calling with your identity. Who we are made to be and what we are made to do are linked because of how God made us, but our purpose is bigger than having a particular career or calling. It is more than fulfilling a specific role. It goes far deeper than completing a set of tasks.

There is a reason we are called human beings instead of human doings. If what we do defines who we are, we've got it backward. Who we are should help us determine what we do, how we live, which career we pursue, and why we are passionate about one thing or another.

Our personalities are formed by many factors including: our upbringing and the beliefs or ideals instilled in us, our life experiences and how we react to those experiences, and the choices we make and the results of those choices. But we are complex beings and are so much more than the sum of our experiences. We have something more than that. We have a purpose mapped in us that we are constantly struggling to understand.

Purpose is a state of being and knowing your heart and mind. It is about discovering your true nature. Are you an encourager, a healer, a comforter, a leader? When we understand our being and why we are the way we are, the doing we choose to focus on will be more powerful and more productive. So, before you try to do more, BE MORE.

If you have something big to overcome, it means your purpose is very big and God is making you stronger! Keep going. Walk in favor.
#BEMORE

SECRET #31
YOU'RE NOT LOOKING FOR AN OUT . . . YOU'RE LOOKING FOR A SOLUTION!

When I tell people to go in a new direction, have faith, and reject fear, some tell me it's not that easy. I don't know if they aren't satisfied with my answer because they want more specific instructions or just want a quick fix. Either way, they are right. It is not that easy. Life is hard. Life takes work. There is no formula for an easy life that you can follow.

I was gang raped in my twenties. I lost a big business in my thirties. I've been falsely accused, judged, and condemned. I've given into my own toxic thoughts that took me onto a path of self-destruction. I've tried to blend in, to settle, and not to make waves.

Yes, life is hard, and there are no easy answers. But the truth is, we don't really want easy. Easy is a Band-Aid. Easy is a cop-out. What we need is a solution, a real change.

There comes a time when you look at the opposition and realize that to stay where you are will be harder to endure than pressing through and taking a bold step in a new direction.

If you're sick of where you've been and something inside of you is telling you that it's time, don't continue looking for an escape from your problem. Look for a resolution. It's not easy to remake your life, nor is it easy to go against the flow. But you are not looking for easy.

You weren't designed to just blend in and you were not created to take the same journey as everyone else. You were created for more. You were designed to walk on water and press through fire—to keep going when everything in you screams that you can't go one more step.

When we ask for easy, what we want is a road already cleared, a ready-made, pre-packaged answer to our struggle. The problem with that is each person is designed uniquely and each solution is unique, so taking that "easy" pre-paved road is going to take us where someone else is going, not where we are supposed to be.

Take your own path. Seek your own answers . . . even if they aren't easy. You were not designed for quick fixes and easy outs. The God of Heaven is there to help you. You were designed for real change. You were designed to BE MORE.

Sometimes we have to get mad at where we currently are in life in order to go somewhere else. Dig deep inside and decide, "No more!"
#BEMORE

SECRET #32
CHANGE YOUR MIND

I meet so many people every single day who know they need to change their lives and yet they don't know how.

Their first mistake is thinking there is one big, global fix to make everything right. It's no wonder they are so lost. Who can figure out where to start when you are looking at such a big job? But, as silly as it sounds, the key is to START. Start by changing how you think. Watch what's going on in your brain every day. Take a closer look at the thoughts that are holding you back and begin changing those. If you are negative all the time, start looking for a positive side. If you are consumed by fear, think of one way you can be brave and build on that. If you hold onto anger and resentment, try to forgive and release one small thing today, then another each day after that.

You can't do this all at once, but you can make a difference by just starting and BELIEVING—really, really believing—that today you are leaving your old life behind. Tell yourself that come hell or high water, no matter what, you will get to your goal.

I was on vacation in Hawaii and was at a famous restaurant and ordered the meal I thought I wanted. Then I had that "food envy" moment where I saw what someone else ordered, and I knew I had to have it. Thankfully, I could just change my order. It was that simple. Changing your mind can be that easy too. You can just choose to have different thoughts.

Don't get me wrong; lasting change does not happen overnight. This kind of healing is a journey. As with all road trips, you won't ever arrive at your destination if you don't get in the car and start the engine. What I mean is that while you may not stop the negative thoughts by flipping a switch, starting that change is as simple as making a single choice every day to keep your mind focused on believing everything God says about you.

Stop putting it off. It's time to begin! To change your life, you have to change your mind. To change your mind, you have to decide you are ready to BE MORE.

Stop thinking so much. Let it go. His strength is made perfect in your weakness, so stop trying to be everything to everyone.
#BEMORE

SECRET #33
HOPE COMES IN THE DARKNESS

We live in a world where sometimes it feels as if everyone is walking around in a daze. We are just going through the motions of life, and we lack hope.

I went through a period when I was really sick and really sad. I was in agony every single day. The pain in my bones and the pain in my heart—the sicknesses I was fighting, the misery over the mistakes I had made, the frustration over trying to live up to everyone else's expectations—were overwhelming and finally took their toll.

But one day a thought came to me: *Look for ways to make things better.*

Trust me, it wasn't a thought from my brain. No way. My brain was a toxic mess back then. God dropped this thought in my head, and my heart felt a tiny penlight-sized glimmer of hope. That flicker of hope caused me to have a few ideas and I wrote them down. This led to another idea, which led to another . . .

A miraculous lightning bolt didn't come down from heaven to rescue me from my mess, but the possibility for relief did fill my heart and my path began to wind down a different road. The notion that things might get better rather than worse was enough to help me keep going, to make me put one foot in front of the other.

Fourteen years later, I am here, miles away from the despair I felt back then. I had no clue this is how much better my "better" would be. I was just hoping to get out of my pit, not to be sick all the time, to live just one day without massive sadness, and to actually do the things I love without pain.

But, God . . . His "better" was so much more. He wanted me to help others out of their dark places, to shine that light of hope on them, and to lead them to a "Better" for greater life than they could imagine.

My friends, look for ways to make things better. Look. Pray. Ask. Write it down. The hope that comes in the darkness is lighting the way for you to BE MORE.

Get ready for new things to happen. Don't fear getting so stuck in the challenges of life that you can't get out. Embrace the change.
#BEMORE

SECRET #34
THE BATTLEFIELD IS IN YOUR MIND

The greatest battle we fight every day is in the mind. The devil attacks it; circumstances manipulate it. Not every thought you have is true.

Every single day you will fight an assaulting terrorist who is after your land. Oddly enough, some of your own "men" will join this assault through memories, distorted perspectives, and other "bad data" stored in your main frame.

Every encounter, situation, comment, song, and TV show you are exposed to is playing constantly in your mind every single second of the day. It's daunting to even think of how many thoughts we each have that we're not consciously aware of. They are shaping our days and who we become.

Think about it for a second. (No pun intended.) Neurologists and psychiatrists and others who study these things have never been able to agree on the exact amount, but they project that the average person has between 40,000 and 70,000 thoughts per day—roughly 40-50 per second. But, how many of those thoughts do we consciously create?

This is how the enemy attacks. He rises in the midst of an already overly busy minefield and wanders virtually unnoticed. It's not every day that the average person will ask themselves, *Are my thoughts obeying my goals? Is that true or is that a lie coming from somewhere in my internal reserves?*

People are groping and struggling to comprehend the meaning behind why they have the thoughts they do and how to get rid of them. In fact, attempting to answer this question has become a multibillion-dollar industry.

The battlefield is in your mind. It is deeply embedded and eventually infects your heart and races through your veins. But the good news is you do not have to be the sum total of every flittering notion that lands on your grey matter.

My friend, take your thoughts captive. Make them obey. Take back control and learn what to ignore, reject, forgive, and release. Have you ever heard of a mantra? That is a saying you can repeat over and over to help your mind focus. When you find yourself dwelling on negative thoughts or feel your mind running away with itself, repeat this verse as your mantra:

> Whatever is true, whatever is noble,
> whatever is right, whatever is pure,
> whatever is lovely, whatever is
> admirable—if anything is excellent or
> praiseworthy—think about such things.
> —Phillipians 4:8

The battlefield is in your mind, but with God in your heart you are more than equipped to win. You are equipped to BE MORE.

Reject the echoes in your head that say you aren't enough and you can't do what God has called you to. In Christ you are powerful!
#BEMORE

SECRET #35
IT DOESN'T HAVE TO BE PERFECT

Perfection is overrated, and perfectionism is a sorry master to serve. We all know we're only 70-80% on our best day anyway, so who are we kidding?

So, you have that room perfect. Nothing is out of place. The room feels settled. You feel peace. I hate to burst your bubble, but it's an illusion—no, I'd even say it is a delusion because the only way this "perfect" room stays that way is if no one ever enters it and it exists in a vacuum. And even then, the notion of perfection is absurd because we can always find some flaw to fix—something that lies below the surface that is not so pristine.

I know personally what it's like to constantly strive for perfection while feeling like a horrible mess inside. The trauma I had experienced as a young girl made me very afraid of disarray. My heart was shattered and my mind was always spinning in pain. It was so much easier to focus on the external messes than it was to deal with all that was going on inside of me.

There were so many days I refused to sit still because if I did stop for a moment I might end up feeling things I didn't want to feel. So I kept moving, pushing, pressing forward to keep things "perfect."

Various things in life would interrupt my pursuit, and then I'd get mad because I didn't feel safe when things didn't go well. It was a long journey overcoming that pathetic lifestyle. It was almost like anxiety and perfection were an addiction and if I didn't get a fix every single day I thought I would die.

When peace took the place of perfection, the room actually began to look brighter. When hope took over hurry, the days began to feel lighter. Every step forward became progress, no matter how big or how small. Staying aware, awake, and alive was now the pursuit. Life, not perfection, was the goal.

Every person in history who has made a significant impact on our culture has also made horrific mistakes and experienced devastating failures. Just remember, there is no such thing as perfect, so you don't have to strive for it. You just have to aim for progress. Live your life, messes and all, and BE MORE.

You don't have to be perfect to go places in life! Just be consistent! Stay on task, be faithful, and you'll get stronger every time!
#BEMORE

SECRET #36
LEARN FROM YOUR MISTAKES

Far too many people can't figure out why their life isn't changing. They make excuses, they allow themselves to take on a victim mindset, and they wallow in self-pity.

The problem is they are making mistakes and they aren't learning from them. Those who feel trapped in a cycle of failure or crisis have not discovered the truth that every mistake holds a lesson.

You are going to make mistakes and you will have failure along the way. As long as you have a pulse, you're going to have challenges. That is part of being human. But the great thing is that mistakes, when viewed the right way, can lead to successes. There is not a single person on this planet who had gotten everything right the first time they tried it. It's just not possible.

Those who are successful and have great lives are the ones who see the opportunity that resides in a mistake and they seize that opportunity and make the most of it. You have to learn to love yourself and give yourself room to mess up so you can grow out of the experience. Know this: every champion has done the same thing.

One of the best ways to grow is to carry a notebook with you and record everything—your successes AND your mistakes. There is so much to learn from everything we go through in life. By writing down these moments and reflecting on them, you will get insights into what you've done right and where you've gone wrong.

If you are making mistakes, it means you are going further than you've gone before. You are stretching your-self and testing yourself. Remember to take good notes along the way so you aren't repeating mistakes.

Don't give up. Don't give in. Don't be afraid and don't limit yourself. Boxes don't hold lives and cages aren't good places to store your dreams. Allow yourself to grow through your struggles so you can BE MORE.

When you hit a speed bump in life, don't get stuck!
Keep your focus forward and look for your next step.
Listen as God leads!
#BEMORE

SECRET #37
BE A CHAMPION

Are you always feeling behind? Do you feel you are always in catch up mode?

Your concern should not be in catching up, but being faithful where you are.

"Catching Up" is a term we use in many aspects of life—in running a race, in our work, in our sleep. But we never realistically "catch up." We just adjust expectations to a new timeline, a new goal, a new state of mind.

Stop stressing and worrying. Stop competing with yourself or others. Stop competing with some arbitrary finish line. Just do your best. Ask yourself daily, *Am I really doing my best?* If the answer is yes, then be at peace and keep moving forward. This is how a champion is made!

I recite this credo when I am tempted to get stressed over getting behind:

> I take full responsibility for my rising and falling.
> I don't beat myself up, nor do I beat up others.
> When I make decisions, I live with the results and don't play a victim.
> With the power that is in me I seek, above all things, wisdom and discernment.
> I fly high and sometimes I crash, but the total race is the goal, not just one stage.
> I know when to push and I know when to pull back.
> I give it my all and I love others even when they don't.
> I am a champion!
> My most powerful words are: I did great and I'll do

better next time!

A champion is far less concerned with whether or not they lose or win every time, and more concerned with doing things with excellence. Whether they are always on top of the leaderboard or come in last place, the true mark of a champion is one who takes on each challenge with the singular goal of doing it to the best of their ability.

We all will fail. We all will miss the mark on occasion. That's okay. It isn't ordained that we will win every race, receive every top award, and defeat everyone who challenges us. No one is that perfect. It is more important to be sure that each time you step onto the field that you have done what you needed to do to be prepared, that you have given this task all your focus, and that you are giving it all you've got.

Step up! Be the Champion our world needs today! BE MORE!

In God's economy 5 fish + 1 boy = 5000 meals.
God doesn't wanna hear about what you don't have.
Give Him what you do have.
#BEMORE

IT'S ASTOUNDING WHAT PEOPLE CAN DO WHEN THEY HAVE SOMEONE WHO BELIEVES IN THEM.

BE MORE . . .

ATTENTIVE TO YOUR RELATIONSHIPS

YOUR TRUEST FRIENDS
ARE THE PEOPLE WHO
DON'T WALK OUT THE
DOOR WHEN LIFE GETS
HARD. THEY ACTUALLY
POUR SOME COFFEE AND
PULL UP A CHAIR.

BE MORE . . .
ATTENTIVE TO YOUR RELATIONSHIPS

What are we in life without our relationships? Our part-
ners, our children, our parents, our friends, our col-
leagues, and even our acquaintances all factor into who
we are and who we become.

Being attentive to these relationships is essential for
our personal growth, as they are a part of our sphere of
influence, which contributes to the work we are here to
do. The way we interact with those in our lives and how
they react to us is a driving force for how effective we are
in what we do each day.

The secrets in this section will help you discover the
depth of impact our relationships have on us and the
way we impact the lives of others. I will remind you of
the significant power of words and how they can speak
life into someone or they can completely destroy their
foundation. We will consider those words in the form of
prayer, encouragement, instruction, inspiration, and even
criticism. How we approach what we say to them can
make all the difference in the world in their success or
failure.

It is also important to consider your actions. Are you
supportive of the dreams your children have? Do you lift
up your partner in their daily efforts? Can you do more to
help others learn from your struggles by sharing the lessons you've learned? Is the example you set one of hard

work, big faith, and enduring optimism?

We were not made to be entirely independent and autonomous. Being more does not happen when our relationships are less than. God made us this way because He wants us to work together in the plans He has for our lives. He also wants relationship with us. I pray that as you draw closer to God and become more aware of yourself, you can grow stronger in your relationships and that all of these layers will work together to deepen your understanding of who you are.

LETTING GO OF THE WRONG PEOPLE IN YOUR LIFE OPENS DOORS FOR THE RIGHT PEOPLE TO SHOW UP!

SECRET #38
CREATE A NURTURING ENVIRONMENT

The people in your inner circle—your family, your friends, and your confidants—are essential to nurturing who you are and who you will become.

As you take this journey toward being more, you will encounter those who are discouraging, critical, unsupportive, and even hurtful. Finding your way to your destiny is not easy. In fact, it can be a really bumpy road at times. Make sure you are surrounding yourself with people who will nurture your growth.

God put a deep yearning to be greater inside of us, and the more we yield to Him, make a commitment to be 100% who He made us to be, the more challenges we will face, because going against the flow is tough. But God is the greatest nurturer there is. There will be times when you feel no one understands you, when it feels like everyone is against you, but this is usually when the greatest growth happens.

If you find you are not getting the support you need from those around you, change your circle. Yes, that's right! Start all over. Change your friends. Create a new social media profile. Stop listening to poison. Ignore your critics.

When you draw your last breath here on earth, you will not be concerned with reading your reviews. You will not summon your loved ones to critique your life. You will be focused on cherishing each moment you have left. So, why would you waste a single moment of any part of your life worrying about other people's opinions?

In all your doing and in all your growing, enjoy every moment that leads up to your last. Chase that fire inside of your belly. You have a gift that should be shared, not hidden by fear of criticism. Build healthy relationships that enrich your life. Choose to surround yourself with people who will encourage, support, and nurture you to BE MORE.

Surround yourself with people who encourage you and lift you up. Life's too short to keep bad company and struggle all day.
#BEMORE

SECRET #39
SET THE RIGHT EXAMPLE

As we aspire to greatness and strive for success, it is easy to neglect our responsibility to those around us.

Working hard is important, and I do not support laziness. I believe in a kingdom-minded work ethic, but there has to be balance. Spending all of your time on building a business or growing a career without giving time to your family and your friends is not healthy either.

Don't kid yourself. You are not "doing it all for them." Being a workaholic doesn't benefit them. And when you let your relationships slide so you can work late, earn a bonus, and keep the boss happy, you are not honoring all God has given you.

Mark my words: If you take care to keep your home life and your work life in balance, God will expand your borders, enlarge your territories, increase your profits, and decrease your stress. You'll sleep better at night and find that champion who has been dormant for too long.

There is nothing better in the world than doing what God has called you to, having your family with you, and working in harmony where everyone grows. When we make right choices, no matter how hard it is, we will receive blessings.

This generation needs people they can look up to. Be one of them. Set the right example for your children, for those who work with or under you, and for those who are on the outside observing your business practices. Keep your priorities straight. Keep yourself and your time balanced so you can BE MORE.

Be someone worth following and looking up to! We need modern-day heroes this generation can look up to! Be real! Be powerful!
#BEMORE

SECRET # 40
LIVE BIG, DREAM BIG

Far too many of us end up living in a refrigerator-box-sized life and have no clue we are holding keys to a mansion.

Too often we keep our lives smaller so we won't be so disappointed. We minimize our goals so we are less likely to fail. We limit our dreams and ourselves so we don't let anyone down. Yet, deep within our DNA is the human desire to expand, go further, and test the limits.

Deep inside all of us is a yearning not only to do more, but to be more as well. So, living timidly and protecting ourselves actually does let someone down. In not pushing ourselves, we are falling short of our potential and short of what God intended for us.

We think we are being responsible and helpful when we tell kids not to get their hopes up, to come down to reality, and to be practical. But we really are doing harm when we don't encourage them to dream—and to dream big. We are cheating them when we don't help them reach for the stars. Mediocrity is not what God planned for us. He made us to do great things.

No, not everyone is made to be a world leader or a celebrity or an innovator, but we are all made with a specific purpose and a drive to fulfill that purpose to the best of our abilities. Settling for the bare minimum of what we can get out of and put into life is not why we are here.

Big dreams are what have enabled the human race to develop throughout history. We would have no advancements in medicine, technology, the arts, government, and all other areas of our cultures without those who dare to push beyond the boundaries of what they can see. The dreamers have grown our communities and made the un-imaginable a reality.

Embrace the natural tendency of children to dream, to imagine anything is possible. Nurture that in your children. Give every member of your family the room to be all they were made to be. Give yourself permission to be great . . . to BE MORE.

Be a cheerleader in people's lives! It's astounding what people can do when they have someone who believes in them and loves them!
#BEMORE

SECRET #41
BE A SOURCE OF GOOD

Do you know your waking thoughts can frame your entire day? Choose wisely where you let your thoughts lead you. Instead of thinking about how tired you are, what undesirable work you have in store, or how little sleep you got, think about the potential the day holds.

What you think about the most is going to multiply and what you think about first will set the tone for where your mind is for the rest of the day. Is this the harvest you want to see in your future? More of what you're thinking about right now? If not, change your mind!

Change the way you approach the day and it will change the way you interact with everyone you encounter. That has a ripple effect. If you are in a negative state of mind, you will dampen the mood and effectiveness of others. But if you are thinking and acting positively, you lift others up and probably improve the direction of their day and the effect they have on those they meet.

Before you can think about impacting others, you have to be aware of how you are letting your environment affect you. If you are not the one who is controlling your mood, others will control your mood for you.

You can either be influenced by everything you encounter throughout the day or you can be the influence. You can be a thermometer reflecting your environment and changing with the temperature of the room, but that is not going to lead you to your purpose. Instead, be a thermostat changing the atmosphere and setting the levels you choose. Take control and be the one who is the change for good.

If you influence one person for good today, you've done

a good work. Make a choice to be the one who makes a real change. You are so much more powerful than you realize. Use that power to make a positive difference in the lives of those you touch each day. Use that power to BE MORE.

You were created to change the world in your generation! If you only touch one person, that person could be the one to change nations!
#BEMORE

SECRET #42
PRAY OVER YOUR CHILDREN AND YOURSELF DAILY

The children we have been trusted to raise will have a direct impact on their communities and the countless other people who will pass through their lives. The words we speak over them will shape who they become.

Some of us grew up hearing things that should never be repeated. Some of us did not receive the outpouring of love and kindness our little souls needed to grow confidently and proudly as children of God. When that happens, there is damage to the core of who we are.

It can take years to begin to realize that we are loved and carefully crafted. Some never realize it and suffer throughout their lives never realizing who they are. Breaking the cycle of pain and woundedness is our responsibility to the next generation.

As parents, we have an enormous responsibility to cultivate healthy spirits in our children. Praying over their lives is a gift to them, to us, and to their future relationships. Because this is so important, I offer this prayer over all of our children:

*I call forth the Lion of the tribe of Judah within you to rise up in courage!
I declare total healing over your mind, your body, your spirit.
Your spirit is perfect in Jesus Christ! Your body, mind, and soul come into alignment now.
All things are coming into wholeness over you and in you. Your mind is brilliant. You have wonderful thoughts.*

You are very wise and accurate in how you think. Your eyes see heaven.
Your spirit and body feel angels and are secure.
Your heart is made perfect in Jesus and you are 100% loved and 100% worthy of all love.
You are a Warrior of the Most High God.
He loves you and accepts you completely.

Speak these affirming words over the children in your life and cultivate a new generation of individuals who know who they are in God and are pursuing their purpose with confidence and clarity. Make a difference for our future and lead others to BE MORE.

God might ask you to break new ground! It might be painful and require endurance, but you will pave a path for future generations!
#BEMORE

SECRET #43
ENCOURAGE AND SUPPORT DREAMERS

Children are the greatest gift God entrusts to us. Not only are we responsible for the safety and wellbeing of another, we also declare and decree over them every day. We mold and shape their lives and influence their choices. We will foster or diminish their destinies depending on what we speak into their lives. Call forth their greatness. Encourage them to dream, and support their goals.

Each of my sons went through a season when they had more time than productive outlets for that time. They weren't focused on anything that would help them move forward in life. During this phase, my typical questions to them were: *What do you want to do? What would you do if you didn't have any limitations?*

It was important to me as their mother to help them explore possibilities without restriction so they could figure out who they were. I now have three very, very successful musicians—a pianist, guitarist, and drummer. My sons are rock stars. Seriously. I'm not just saying that because I am their mom. Unbiased observers also tell them, "You are gifted for that."

My sons are happily pursuing fulfilling careers—a videographer, a film maker, a hunter, a dreamer, a wild boy—and being the individuals they were created to be. One double checks everything while another flows through life so freely he forgets to pick up his clothes more times than not. They were *designed* to be this way and it is my job as their mother to encourage and support their unique paths.

If we train up a child in the way they *should* go—not in the way you *want* them to go or the public education system instructs them to go or the way society dictates they are supposed to go—they will become adults who contribute positively to their world and touch lives around them in encouraging and supportive ways, continuing the cycle.

Take the opportunity you have as a parent to make a difference in your child's life. Declare favor from God over your children. Decree a future with limitless possibilities.

Learn to dream for yourself by dreaming with your kids. As you help them find their way, you just might find your own way to BE MORE.

Have a dream that takes you beyond where you are now. Get in over your head! Dream so big it's beyond you and God has to show up!
#BEMORE

SECRET #44
EQUIP OTHERS FOR GREATNESS THEN GET OUT OF GOD'S WAY

Have you ever noticed how we tend to tell people to strive for greatness as the people of God, but when they embrace those gifts we turn on them and accuse them of being vain, overly ambitious, worldly, or even sinful?

We instruct and pray for Christians to invade the marketplace, bringing the love of God to everyone throughout the world, but once they are there being the salt and light we sent them to be, the criticism begins to fly. They are too focused on the world and not enough on the church. They have forgotten their foundation. They are being influenced rather than being the influence.

We have to be mindful of the judgments we are placing on the successes of others. If God has called them to work in a high-profile position, it is our responsibility to equip them for success in this calling and get out of God's way as He continues that work through them. If God raises up someone in Hollywood or Las Vegas or Washington, we must be very careful to support them in prayer and encouragement, and we must not give in to jealousy and the temptation to tear them down. We cannot comprehend what God is doing there. We cannot know what work He is performing through them.

When we train our children for greatness, we must prepare them, empower them, and equip them to be great, powerful, and holy. Equip them to trust where God has placed them and what He has planned for them.

We do not have insight into the ways God chooses to move and use us for His purposes. Don't criticize what you don't understand. Just allow God to move through you, through others, and through circumstance without interfering. When you get out of the way, prepare to see God's greatness in yourself, in your children, and in others. Prepare to BE MORE.

If you feel called to change the world and make a big impact, be prepared for people to either love you or hate you.
#BEMORE

SECRET #45
LET YOUR CHALLENGES FUEL YOUR PASSION

Isn't it interesting how the very thing we are terrified of is many times directly attached to the thing we're called to? What is a calling anyway? Do you hear a voice, follow it, and know you've been "called?"

Maybe it is more like a burning flame inside your soul that won't let up and won't go away no matter how you might try to ignore it. It is the kind of flame that continues to smolder even when you don't tend it.

What flame burns inside of you? What is that thing you dreamed of as a child? Perhaps someone told you to put it away because it had no place in the real world. I am here to apologize for that lack of encouragement and to tell you right now to fan that flame that had died down. Rekindle the passion that burns slowly, deep in your heart.

There is no room for practical when you are pursuing the passion God has given you. What if someone had told Jackie Robinson or Billie Jean King to be practical as they trained daily, pushing their bodies and the boundaries in their fields? What if someone had told Steve Jobs or Bill Gates to think realistically as they sought to expand the realm of possibility in technology, giving us what seemed like fantasy to use in our everyday lives?

Imagine if someone had told them they couldn't dream that big and they had listened! Spend some time reclaiming your drive, your passion. Where does your fire take you? What does it inspire you to do for yourself and others?

Fuel the flames of your passion because you never know how it will make a difference in the way another person pursues their greatness. Be passionate and driven.

Be an inspiration. BE MORE.

The size of the opposition against you might reflect the enormity of your calling! Let the challenge fuel your passion.
#BEMORE

SECRET #46
USE YOUR STRUGGLES TO IMPROVE SOMEONE ELSE'S LIFE

Many of you have lived your entire lives struggling to have enough. Maybe you endured a difficult childhood, watching your parents fight to make ends meet, learning that you would never have what others did, and accepting the brutal fact that life would always involve hardship. You became all too familiar with insufficiency. You learned that money worries were just a way of life. You embraced lack as a normal state.

While material things are not the true test of your worth, living in constant "survival mode" does not leave room for dreaming. It does not allow time for growth. Living under such hardship can crush the dreamer's spirit, and those who have important roles to fulfill in God's plan may not realize them because they are inhibited by the pressure of getting through the day.

This is no way to live and certainly no way to become the champion God wants you to be. There is so much more to life than being stuck in need. While your financial situation may not change over night, your attitude about it does. Although you may not receive miraculous healing for your soul wounds in a moment, your outlook on how you walk through life can get better.

This state of wanting and needing that is holding you back may come in many forms, but you can begin to reverse it by believing in the truth that God made you for something very special and wants great things for you. Today, right now, I break that spirit of poverty off of you. I release "there is enough" and "YOU are enough" into your life. I release great grace over you and pray you discover a childlike heart to work hard, trust your Heavenly Father, and receive His blessings.

The false belief that you won't receive any blessing is gone now. The need to say nothing works for you and you will always struggle is cast out. I pray you will see how important you are and that you will shift your thinking. Receive God's promises with full belief.

Release these words into your life and then go impact someone else with the same truths.

Add value to everyone you encounter on a daily basis. But, to do this, you first need to see and believe how valuable YOU really are.
#BEMORE

SECRET #47
TRUST THE DREAM GOD GAVE YOU

Why do people criticize other people's dreams? What fear leads them to discourage others from trying to be their best, from trying to be all God made them to be?

There is an old English proverb that says, "When a proud man hears another praised, he feels himself injured." Don't let the jealousy and insecurity of others distract you from pursuing the dream God put in your heart.

Your dreams are part of a bigger picture, and God might be trying to do something in the world that needs to be done for us all. Think about it! That vision you keep getting isn't just about you! Oh sure, you're the "vessel." You are the pioneer who has been chosen. But it's not all about you. You are a tool in the grand workroom of life, and God is trying to love us all through what he does in your life.

So, if a critic comes and we are challenged, we may begin to question who we are—the validity of our dreams and the truth in what we're attempting to achieve. Don't let those words be a distraction. When critics come and make fun of your dreams and your desire to be more, forgive them. Shrug it off, and then dream bigger.

Forgiveness is critical for dreamers. If we don't learn to forgive and release, we'll never see our dreams come true. The opinions of our critics and why they are putting down our dreams are not important.

Remind yourself: *I forgive my critics. I have God's approval and that is all that matters. Their heart must be so small or so broken that I threaten them. I pray they find out who God made them to be.*

You've got a purpose to fulfill! Be inspired. Get motivated. Dream bigger and BE MORE.

Your biggest dream could be a part of something God
wants to release in the world!
Please, don't give up!
#BEMORE

SECRET #48
BE TRUE TO YOU

A continual theme throughout these secrets is to remind you that you were created with a unique design and it's your job to make sure you fulfill that purpose! But there's something I must address. Being true to yourself does not mean you have to hate others. It does not mean you need to pick fights or rant about everything.

You do not have to live your life on a soapbox. Sometimes the best way to be true to yourself is to keep your comments to yourself. Far too many people are completely insecure about who they are, what they stand for, and where they are going in life. As a result, what we find is a bunch of people perpetually in "defense" mode. They are constantly trying to argue their positions and make their case.

Take a quick look at Facebook. How many posts are from someone who feels they are not being heard, giving a piece of their mind to a captive audience? They get worked up over the issue of the day and, by ranting to their friends, aren't likely to reach the audience that is supposedly in need of these lessons. Productive conversations that can change hearts and minds do not happen in that forum. All you are accomplishing by this practice is getting yourself bothered and distracted from more productive activities.

This is not being true to yourself or your purpose. In fact, you could be undoing your influence by alienating people. You have a more powerful impact through what you do rather than what you say. How you live your life, how you conduct yourself, how you pursue your purpose, and how you hold to your principles influences more people than a well-worded Facebook post or blog reply ever will. It comes down to how you're living your life.

The two secrets I learned in business that have held me through many trials and successes are ignoring my critics and my competitors and staying true to myself—this includes having pink hair and tattoos, and not censoring myself based on what others think I should say. It comes down to being true to myself and honoring who I believe God made me to be.

So, how will you live? How will you strive to BE MORE?

Quit telling me what you don't believe in or what you don't agree with! Tell me what you do believe in! Tell me about your dreams!
#BEMORE

SECRET #49
YOUR SUCCESS IS ABOUT YOU

Too many of our dreams are derailed because we are too focused on what others have to say about them.

We wonder why they can't be more supportive. We begin to question our choices. We worry they might know something we don't and allow that to grow into fear. The truth is fear is most likely what is driving their comments. Sometimes they are threatened by your big dreams because they are coming face to face with the reality that you are going somewhere and they are not. Some might even be afraid you are going somewhere without them!

Don't fall into codependent behavior—feeling like you have to get everyone else's approval so you can pursue your dreams. Remember that the biggest pain point we all have in our lives is what we see in the mirror, and we rarely want to deal with that. Instead, we turn on others who, through their own progress and personal growth, make us look at what is in that mirror we've been trying to avoid.

There was a time in my life when I was the only person who had a vision for being more and changing everything. God made me to be a THERMOSTAT: I regulate things around me. Whether I like it or not, my gifting is to influence people. I remember telling God one day, "Can't I have a bad day on my own? Why can't I have a fit when no one else has to have a fit too?" He said, "No." The gifts He gave me were intended to impact the world, so my attitude, my countenance, and my dreaming (or lack thereof) were going to influence people around me.

That is when I decided to be who God made me to be, to reject the negative noise, the condemning voices, and to release the heartache of my past. Initially people thought it was a "phase" and some even thought I was delusional. Now, I'm the one influencing millions. It's not an easy path, but it's so right. It's so worth it.

You are going to have to develop a tough skin, and you are going to have to forgive a lot on this journey. People won't understand. People will be critical and cruel. But God knows. God loves and supports. Lean into Him. Draw close to those who get it and remember your success is about you and what God is doing through you.

Be brave. Be bold. BE MORE.

Quit trying to change everyone around you so you can feel like you deserve success.
They have nothing to do with it! It's Y-O-U!
#BEMORE

SECRET #50
DON'T BACK AWAY FROM THE TOUGH STUFF

Being positive and living a life that is powerful doesn't mean everything will always be happy or easy.

We are not promised a life free from struggle or strife. Some of the most rewarding experiences we will have in life come with the price of hard work, difficult encounters, and painful choices.

There are times in my life as a business owner when I need to ask an employee to account for poor performance. There are moments in my marriage when my husband and I have to talk about hard things. There have been periods as a parent when I have to confront my children about their behavior. During these times I need the wisdom of heaven, the love of an accepting God, and the fortitude of a Champion.

I will face difficult choices, things that make me uncomfortable, and decisions that are scary. And yes, even things I absolutely hate to do. I will have to take on all of these to get the kind of life I am dreaming of.

Responsibility. Accountability. Wisdom. They are big words and tough to live by. They are nearly super powers in this age. But, when combined with joy, hope, and love, they will take you farther, help you last longer, and create better relationships.

We have to do hard things to live powerfully. We cannot avoid the tough stuff if we want anything in life that is truly worthwhile. We don't get to behave like cowards and expect to become champions. If greatness came easy, it wouldn't have any significance. If everyone could do it, it wouldn't be special.

Life is messy. We don't all get along all the time. Even

the most caring people with the best of intentions make mistakes and hurt those they love. The right thing isn't always what we choose. So, we have to have grace. We have to have forgiveness. We have to have courage to take on the tough stuff. We have to work hard to BE MORE.

People learn by what we do, not by what we say. Being a leader doesn't mean you're perfect, but it does mean your life is an example!
#BEMORE

SECRET #51
HOLD YOUR TONGUE

The wisest among us are those who have opinions and the discernment to know when to share them and when to keep quiet.

We all encounter things we disagree with, and that's okay, but we don't have to launch a big discussion about every issue that comes up. It is important to know when your comments will be useful and when they add nothing to a conversation. We also need to know when they only serve as a distraction from something else that really needs your attention.

It is easy for us to throw in our two cents at every opportunity, especially in the world of social media and blogging. Everyone has a platform from which to speak now. That does not mean they should. And, in most cases, we are not giving any real thought to what we put out there. We open our mouths or we start typing without using our God-given ability to filter and decide if what we are saying really needs saying.

There is a time and a place for things and tasks to be fulfilled—a moment at hand, a calling in front of you. If the opinion you are about to offer does not support, enhance, or otherwise benefit your purpose, reconsider putting it out there.

A wise man once said, "It is better to remain silent and be presumed an idiot than to open your mouth and remove all doubt." Now, I'm not calling anyone an idiot, but a lot of times, when we choose not to hold our tongues it can be a really dumb move.

Think before you speak. Think about whether express-ing your opinion will benefit or distract you. Think about how it will or will not align with your purpose. Think about whether or not it will help you to BE MORE.

Be the shocking one who doesn't need to have the last word. Don't pay back. Don't get even! Be different! Be bigger!
#BEMORE

SECRET #52
LET IT GO

It is so easy to get sucked into believing the negative messages that swirl around us. We are so susceptible to self-doubt, which can lead to doubting God's love for us. But God isn't tolerating us; He celebrates us.

Zephaniah 3:17 says, "The Lord your God is in your midst, a mighty one who will save; he will rejoice over you with gladness; he will quiet you by his love; he will exult over you with loud singing."

I am so sorry if people in your life have made you feel as if you were not even worth tolerating, let alone loving. What you need to realize is they were projecting their own stuff onto you. It's a lie.

I suffered a terrible trauma as a child, and in my twenties I was gang raped. As a young mother I also endured horrible and unfair treatment in very ungodly churches. These cruelties we inflict on each other all come from a place of personal pain and brokenness. And we need to find the freedom to release this pain for good. God has given you the free will to choose to do that. It's your choice.

We cling to past hurts expecting an apology to come. We don't extend forgiveness because we are waiting for a confession. But you don't need the offender to admit it was hurtful, violent, abusive, or that it tore you to shreds before letting it go. It is your decision to live in the misery or to live free from it.

While you will never forget, you can learn how to keep yourself from dwelling on it every single day. You can find relief from the anxiety, fear, and panic. The torment can leave your body right now.

You are worth it. Jesus believed you were worth dying for. You can be free. In your heart. In your mind. Right now. Ask Him to forgive you. Receive His forgiveness. Cancel the pain. Cancel the torment. Cancel the suffering. You won't walk through it alone, because God is not tolerating you. He loves you.

I don't care what anyone else has told you, I am telling you right now—no matter what has happened, what you've done, no matter how often you've done it, no matter what it is—you matter. You are worth it and you deserve to be free. Set yourself free to BE MORE.

To advance in the Kingdom of God, be humble, quickly forgive, and don't be bitter. Work on your own stuff; don't worry about others.
#BEMORE

SECRET #53
NO MORE NEGATIVE SPEECH

The words we speak become our future. What you say will become the way you live your life. Life or death, we have power. We create.

Listen to yourself. Try making a recording. I know it can be pretty embarrassing, but try it. Take your smartphone and record yourself for the first two hours of the day. Later in the day, play it back to yourself.

When I did this it was a rude awakening. I felt the barometric pressure around me change. "This is my life?" I asked myself. The two hours were filled with: "I'm so sick and tired of this!" and "God has made a great mistake and this is so unfair. No matter how hard I try I can't get ahead!" and "I can't do this. Seriously, who the hell does God think I am anyway?" (Yes, I said hell and God in one sentence and He didn't strike me. Keep reading.)

For all 1 million+ of you on social media who turn to me for inspiration, motivation, and encouragement every single day of the year, this is how I used to talk—used to—until I made a decision to pay attention to the words I was saying. But it wasn't easy. Losing sixty pounds was easier. The words coming out of my mouth were ruining my life, and I had to get control of them.

So what did I do? I looked at the mess I was in and the past I had lived and just decided to change. Then I played pretend. You know, like kids do. I pretended I was happy. I didn't fake it; I just imagined it, like a little girl who plays princess. I began to think about how I would feel once things changed and what my emotions and words would be like once things were different. And then I began to talk like that.

Even today, there are days when the devil is waiting for me by the coffee pot and is attempting to take over my mind and capture my emotions. I respond with, "Now, now, that's not who I am. That's just who I used to be."

The words we say are creative. They aren't just going into thin air and evaporating! Think about what the Bible says about the power of words. They are so powerful that God didn't wave a magic wand or perform a chemical reaction to create the universe and everything in it. He spoke it into being.

Be mindful of what you speak into your life. Use positive, affirming speech. Speak life into your day. Speak the power to BE MORE.

Shout down the negative voices in your head.
Stop wallowing in self-pity and buying into their lies.
Receive all God planned for you!
#BEMORE

WE ARE CALLED TO
RELEASE LIFE, CHANGE
CULTURES, TRANSFORM
ATMOSPHERES, AND
BELIEVE THE BEST EVEN
WHEN THE BEST DOESN'T
LOOK POSSIBLE.

BE MORE . . .

ENGAGED WITH YOUR
COMMUNITY

SPEAK TO PEOPLE'S DESTINY. SEE WHAT GOD SEES. DECLARE IT, CALL IT OUT TO THEM! BE A LIBERATOR AND FREEDOM CREATOR!

BE MORE . . .
ENGAGED WITH YOUR COMMUNITY

I am sure by now you've heard the saying, "It takes a whole village to raise a child." It is an old African proverb that means society does not function well without cooperation from everyone. We are all made with a specific calling and equipped with special gifts. That tells us two things: 1) We have a special part to play in life that no one else can fulfill, and 2) we were not meant to do everything alone.

Living in community holds great benefits and great responsibilities. We are not entirely self-sufficient, no matter how much we'd like to think we are. We need to rely on the person who is gifted with educating to teach our children. We have to call on the person who has the talent of craftsmanship to build our shelters and furniture. We need the person who was given the knowledge of agriculture to grow our food. We need them so we can do what we were called to do without having to struggle in areas that aren't our gifting to meet our daily needs.

How we engage with our community is a crucial part of being more. The secrets in this section will cover our responsibilities to our communities including how we use our influence, how we choose which battles to fight, and how we leave a mark on the place where we live.

We will also discover secrets about the ways community benefits us such as the support we get for realizing our dreams, the opportunities that come in working together instead of against one another, and the freedom that comes in understanding and celebrating everyone's differences.

I pray you will find your place in community and be enriched by those around you as you figure out what role you are to play to make it stronger. I pray you will become uniquely you as you become part of a larger group.

IT ONLY TAKES A SMALL
SPARK TO START A FLAME.
BE THAT SPARK OF HOPE.

SECRET #54
USE YOUR INFLUENCE RESPONSIBLY

More than 4.8 billion times per day someone clicks the "Like" button on Facebook. Hundreds of millions of tweets are posted every twenty-four hours on Twitter. Social media never sleeps.

Behind every smart phone, pad device, laptop, and desktop computer sits a person with a story and a dream. Many are heartbroken. Many are shattered. They feel imprisoned by negative influences that surround them every day. They often turn to the internet, seeking a way out of the darkness. Social media can be a lifeline for people who feel lost.

Never underestimate the power of your words and actions online and through social media. With a few kind words, you can change a person's life. There might be someone out there in despair, and then your tweet or post comes through and suddenly they feel a little more connected and a little less alone.

Every single week I hear from someone sharing how something I posted on social media helped them to go on one more day—people confessing they were at their end. Literally. Some have said they were going to commit suicide when one post changed everything.

Do you have any idea how influential you could be in one person's life today? More than that, do you have any idea how much the enemy of your soul wants you to remain silent?

Those distractions, discouragements, and negative thoughts that bombard your mind are part of the enemy's plan to silence you so you can't bring help or healing to anyone else.

Think about how the things people say can affect the tone of your entire day if you take the thoughts or words to heart as truth. The same is true for what *you* say to others. One word, one post, and one video clip by you could change everything for them.

Do not let the enemy muzzle you. Use your voice in a positive, uplifting way. You were created to be a part of a bigger plan, and your purpose is a necessary piece of that picture.

That picture you felt led to post, that funny thought that came flittering through your mind, those processings and ponderings you've written in your journal for your eyes only—any of these might be a key for all the world to see change.

Use your influence responsibly. Be an inspiration to others so we can all BE MORE.

Sometimes we have to go through things now so we can have an incredible life later! Be willing. Have endurance! Go through it!
#BEMORE

SECRET #55
USE YOUR WORDS FOR GOOD

Our tongue is a ready writer. We have the power to wound and to heal by the words we speak. While these words might not be stored in a database forever, they are written in heaven and there is an account of how they impact the world.

The greatest creations God ever made were you and me. Speak kindly about His children because your words reveal what you think of God and what you think of yourself. Let the words you speak mirror the life you want to live.

When we criticize and judge, we are tearing down this beautiful creation, treating it with no care or value.

Do you know what "cutting" is? It is a trend in young people where they inflict physical wounds on themselves in an attempt to distract themselves from the deep, emotional pain they are experiencing. We live in a time when millions of people are verbal cutters. Their tongue is their knife and they cut and cut and cut. They are hemorrhaging from the repeated lashes they give themselves. Then they go cut other people.

It is a vicious cycle of hurting ourselves and hurting others who go and do the same. Our tongues are writing our futures, and we are not on a good path when we use such hurtful speech. But you can start anew no matter where you are, no matter what you've been through.

I've been through some deep darkness in my past, and I've beat myself up so many times, my own hands have created scars deeper than anyone else ever could have done. When I began to use my own mouth, my own mind, and my own heart to speak kindness and encouragement over myself, I came upon this amazing thought:

No one can take this away from me.

No one can diminish my value with words as long as the words I speak over myself are in agreement with the words of love and grace God is speaking over me.

Use your words for good. Use your words to bring healing and to help others BE MORE.

See the bright side and the possibilities in all situations. It will completely change you and your life!
#BEMORE

SECRET #56
KINDNESS IS THE BEST CURRENCY

Kindness can seem like a rare commodity these days. Even basic courtesy can get lost in the rush and flurry of our lives.

Without mindful kindness, our competitive natures allow us to run right over others in our way. Without intentional kindness, our insecurities become overblown and we lash out in cruelty. Without active kindness, our instinct for self-preservation leads us to disregard the needs of others in favor of our own. Kindness is necessary to temper our lesser selves and keep them from escalating difficult situations.

When people go out of their way to try to discredit me on a blog post without taking ownership of their comments, it makes me wonder: *Are they not being heard at home?* Maybe they don't know who they are. I could get angry and defensive. I could let it unsettle me and make me doubt myself. But that also is not kind . . . to either of us.

Choose kindness. That doesn't mean you become a doormat and make all the sacrifices. It just means you give more when no one expects you to. You mindfully, intentionally, and actively choose to extend mercy, avoiding retaliation or retribution.

Kindness is currency that has a multiplying exchange. The more you give away, the more you get back. The best way to inspire kindness is to smile often. I'm convinced that a smile not only has a benefit for the person who will wear one (ever tried to be depressed when you were genuinely smiling?), but it also has an impact on everyone who sees you smile. Don't know what to say? Pause.

Smile. Feel unkind words coming to the surface? Give it a rest. Smile instead.

Love everyone—not just the ones you agree with or the ones you can support, and not just the ones who are easy to love. After all, God so loved the entire world that He gave His only Son, Jesus. Don't be confused by those who would have you believe God only loved a select few and the rest are doomed. Ignore that lie.

He loves the darkest stranger, the vilest criminal, and the most radical religious nutcase. He loves all of his creation—young and old, wise and clueless, rich and poor, good and bad—and He sent Jesus for all of us.

Jesus was the embodiment of kindness, turning the other cheek, loving unconditionally, forgiving completely, and taking on all of our burdens. Be like Jesus. Be kind. BE MORE.

Working to get along with people will make you strong. Living in agreement with people creates a powerful team!
#BEMORE

SECRET #57
GOD MAKES A WAY WHERE WE SEE NONE

Far too many people who call themselves Christians are so afraid of the devil that they never reach into the darkness to bring light. Evil has such a stronghold in this world because most of us are too scared to go where we are really needed to spread God's love.

If we have any hope of changing the lives of those in need of God's grace, we have to find the courage to go into the dark places. Strengthen your faith. Set aside agendas and formulas for salvation. Forget about all of the instructions and warnings. Just go with one motive—to love, and I mean *really* love—and the rest will take care of itself.

People are shattered by life. They need to know Jesus Christ holds the healing they are so desperately seeking in all the wrong places. You can lead them to the answer, but hiding in your self-protective tiny bubble isn't helping anyone!

Press in and do what most won't do. Go where most won't go. That is exactly where Jesus led His Dirty Dozen to minister! I refer to them as the "Dirty Dozen" because they were all a mess when they met Him! They were unqualified and full of their own crap, yet Jesus enabled, empowered, and equipped them!

The twelve Jesus called never would have been asked to join an advisory board or be elders. They were fishermen and trade workers, not leaders or scholars with religious training.

Heck! Peter was so insecure he had a hard time taking a stand on anything; John had a fierce temper; Matthew was a much-hated tax collector; and Judas . . . well, we know all too well what his faults were.

Though these twelve men were flawed and fearful, confused and impulsive, they turned the world upside down, spreading the love of Jesus, and they did it with limited resources. Think of how much more you and I can do today with all we have at our disposal. Who are you and whose are you? Rise up mighty warrior! Go out into your world and bring light into the dark places. Go BE MORE!

The tougher your circumstances, the bigger your victory can be! When God is at work, the whole is greater than the sum of the parts.
#BEMORE

SECRET #58
PICK YOUR BATTLES

With so many people, responsibilities, and demands competing for our attention, it is important to know what to ignore. Some things don't deserve our time or the energy it takes to give a response.

You don't have to comment on every one of your friends' Facebook posts. Every tweet that includes @yourname doesn't require a reply or even further thought. Having social integrity doesn't mean you should allow yourself to be drawn into heated conversations with people who are a little too coo-coo for Cocoa Puffs over issues that don't really matter.

The ability to ignore what doesn't enhance your life is called discernment. We get to choose where we focus our mental, physical, and emotional energies. God gave us discernment to help us determine what deserves our attention and what does not.

If you want to go places in life, you'll need to learn how to discern whether something is bringing what God intended for you today or if it is a distraction. It is important to pick your battles—choose carefully which challenges you take on. Sometimes you do need to correct misconceptions, guard your reputation, and mend fences. When you are letting God lead you, you will know what really is worth your time.

And here's another secret:

Not all things positive are helpful. Time with friends, time for yourself, and time with family are all positive ways to enjoy and enrich your life. BUT that doesn't mean they are the right areas to focus your energies or spend your time all the time, especially if they distract you from other responsibilities that make the time with them possible. Things don't have to be unhealthy or destructive to be negative influences on our focus and energy.

So, make wise decisions about what gets your focus every day. Give your energy to people, activities, and thoughts that affirm who you are and where you are going. Let discernment guide your steps and help you to BE MORE.

Success is not a mystery. It's not luck. It's the outworking of repeated right choices and decisions even when difficulties come.
#BEMORE

SECRET #59
GO THE EXTRA MILE

What do you do when you know God is calling you to go the extra mile but you're afraid of all the potential detours along the way?

It helps to keep in mind that going the extra mile, doing something no one asked you to do, and being more than anyone expected you to be will not only help others, it will change you for the better as well.

Our character grows when we go above and beyond. God doesn't ask us to turn the other cheek, go the extra mile, or give someone the benefit of the doubt because he is favoring them. He does it because he loves us and wants us to be the best we can be, and that only happens when we can get outside of ourselves and put the needs of others above our own at times.

As I communicate with hundreds of thousands of people every single day on social media, I find that one of the big detours many of them fear getting caught up in is codependency when turning the other cheek.

Here are a few clues to know the difference and avoid the detour:

- I am codependent when I work on your goals more than you work on your goals.
- I am codependent when I do something for you because it makes me feel great, not because you will feel great.
- I am codependent when I go the extra mile for you and then passive-aggressively complain about it.

Going the extra mile means truly not expecting anything in return. It means accepting the possibility you will never receive recognition or thanks for what you've done. It means having a 100% pure heart in your actions.

Another potential detour is becoming so self-sacrificing that you lose sight of your own needs and give to your own detriment. There is a delicate balance between our call to die to self and giving until you have nothing left to give. It is about balance.

God wants us to consider the needs of others so we can grow beyond our selfish tendencies, but we also need to be sure we are tending to our personal growth and nurturing ourselves to replenish what we give out.

We are of no help to anyone if we don't have our house in order. If you don't take care, trying to go the extra mile can further burden the person you are trying to help or put an unnecessary burden on someone else.

As with any path worth taking, there will be difficult legs of the journey. Trust God to lead you as you go the extra mile. But don't be afraid to take that step to BE MORE.

Go the extra mile. Be hot, not lukewarm. When others give up, keep moving! You'll claim the prize when others faint!
#BEMORE

SECRET #60
WE REAP WHAT WE SOW

You've probably heard the saying, "Grace is getting what you don't deserve. Mercy is not getting what you do deserve."

When we take time to realize how kind God has been to us—I don't mean the time we got a great parking spot and had more money in the bank and everything went our way; I mean on the days when we really blow it and He's still kind—this is when it is easy to understand that saying and hard to believe how enduringly true it is.

It is also hard in these moments of awareness to understand why we are so often incapable of giving the same to others in our lives. We are more likely to have days when we don't take responsibility and when we're not being our best self. We know we aren't doing what we should; yet God loves us. So, why are we withholding that kindness from others?

When we are kind to others though they don't deserve it, expect it, or really understand it, we partner with God in a way that not only shows His love to the world, but also sets in motion a positive cycle of sowing and reaping. When we extend grace and mercy to others, they are more likely to give that back to us when we need it and offer it to others they encounter.

We have great power to cultivate positive or negative experiences and attitudes. It all depends on what we put out there to grow in the lives of others.

If we plant seeds of bitterness, anger, unforgiveness, and hatred, we will harvest difficult relationships, hurtful experiences, unhappy homes, and unproductive lives. When we sow kindness, joy, grace, and love, we will reap healthy families, strong friendships, personal growth, support for our dreams, and a better world.

Be mindful of what you put out there as you live, work, play, and love. Give people grace and mercy for their human failings, and lift them up to be better and to BE MORE.

The way we treat others reveals how we want to be treated. If we're responsible and respectful, it's amazing what comes back to us!
#BEMORE

SECRET #61
TRIM THE DEAD WEIGHT TO MAKE ROOM FOR GROWTH

Expansion. People of faith pray for this all the time.

We ask God to enlarge our territories and expand our borders, but so often we are not prepared for that growth. We may be asking God to squeeze a 4,500-square-foot lifestyle into a 1,000-square-foot space. There are times when, in order to expand and grow, we might need to give up a few things. We will need to make more room for what God wants to give us.

This means letting go of the things that fill our time and our minds that currently are not contributing to our expansion. Say goodbye to your exhausting habits—the pretending to be something you are not, the unrealistic expectations you place on yourself or others, your distracted and unfocused energy. Set boundaries in your relationships and limit the access people have to you and your time if they are not building you up and supporting your growth.

Purge the useless things taking up space. Get rid of the strongholds that keep you bound in unhealthy cycles and confined to that 1,000 sq. feet of limited life. Prune the unhealthy stuff from your life so you can flourish. That is how you will become the best version of yourself.

Expansion takes work, and growth doesn't come without growing pains. Remember how your joints ached when you were young as you were going through a growth spurt? You wouldn't stop that growth just because it hurt a little? So don't shy away from spiritual growth just because there is some pain involved. You know the outcome is worth it.

When you are free to expand, you will become all God

planned for you to be and lives will be changed. You will be empowered to really make a difference.

You are going to have to expand so God can do more through you if you want to reach the level of excellence that allows you to BE MORE.

Be the best example you can be. Let excellence, not perfection, be your goal. The world needs people worth following.
#BEMORE

SECRET #62
DON'T BECOME APATHETIC

It is so easy to get stuck in a rut. Even when we are unhappy, we can get comfortable with that state.

Sometimes we are being lazy and don't want to put in the work to break free. Sometimes we are scared and are paralyzed by the fear of the unknown. Maybe we feel clueless and don't know which direction to move. It could be that we have become apathetic and aren't bothered enough by the state of things to put forth the effort to change.

I guess it's like they say, the devil you know is better than the one you don't know. You may not be where you want to be, but it is familiar and that makes it safe. Stretching beyond this comfort zone—even if it is to reach for something far greater and more rewarding—requires a leap of faith. For those who have grown complacent, this is a risk that just doesn't seem worthwhile. They will wallow in mediocrity, unconcerned about the part they are supposed to be playing in God's plan or the impact not doing that can have on everyone around them.

It takes something drastic and dramatic to shake them loose from their apathy. Only when the inconvenience that comes from staying where they are is greater than the inconvenience of moving forward will they make the change. Sadly, some people can be so okay with being uncomfortable that having a better life isn't appealing to them until it is more inconvenient to stay stuck.

Apathy is a thief of ambition, a stealer of dreams. It drains our motivation and drive. It squelches our passion and distracts us from our purpose. Don't let yourself become apathetic. Keep yourself focused on the potential tomorrow holds. Cling to the excitement that comes from discovering new things.

If you are already stuck there, try to do one new thing each day. Break your routine in some way every chance you get and catch the vision for what lies ahead.

Give yourself a chance to try something new. Give yourself a chance to BE MORE.

We won't ever leave where we are until we decide that we'd rather be somewhere else. Make a decision and then do the work!
#BE MORE

SECRET #63
TAKE CHANCES ON OTHERS, ON YOURSELF, AND ON GOD

Have you ever had someone ask you how you are doing and you responded with "Oh, staying busy," or "I have so much to do right now!"? Isn't that a strange response?

Every day people are trying to do more. We have schedules for this, planners for that, and timers to help us wring every minute out of the day until the next thing we know we are penciling in our bathroom breaks! Doing more doesn't make you more; it just makes you more tired.

The real goal is to be more. God is far more interested in who we become, who we do life with, and how we end up. The thing is, as we focus on being more—looking into our hearts and seeing what we need to fix so we can be a blessing to more people—God will accomplish something we never expected. Ironically, we'll end up doing more because we are now working with God rather than against His plan.

When our focus is on others and how to serve them and add value to them, it's incredible how valuable we become. When our prosperity is driven by how generous we can be, it's amazing how rich we become!

The thoughts of God toward you are higher than man's thoughts, higher than the enemies thoughts!

If you are in Christ, He has seated you in heavenly places at the same time that you are walking on the earth, and heaven calls for you to think higher thoughts, to be more, and to go farther than you ever could on your own.

Instead of worrying about maximizing your productivity, consider maximizing your faith. Don't concern yourself so much with filling up your To Do list. Give your energy to a fulfilling purpose.

Today, think higher. Think as God thinks. See possibility in very dark places. See potential in people who seem to have given up. Turn your attention to where God wants you to devote your time. Stop just being busy so you can BE MORE.

God asks us to take risks and promises to go through it with us! Our mistakes don't ruin His odds. He knows how to clean up a mess!
#BEMORE

SECRET #64
DON'T CONCERN YOURSELF WITH CONFORMITY

Okay, once and for all, can we stop trying to be normal? I mean, seriously, who got to decide what is "normal" and made that the be-all-end-all for us anyway?

Who started this game we play, constantly comparing ourselves with society's definition of "normal"? We are so afraid of standing out that we have made conformity an ideal, and even when we try to be a little unconventional, we end up doing "different" the same way.

But God didn't make any of us alike. All the way down to our DNA, we are unique. We might have similarities and we might find interests in common, but we are not made to be exact copies of each other.

Why would we *want* to be cookie-cutter versions of every one else? Sure, there is some comfort in having similarities and feeling connected, but since none of us were made to be the same and all of us have unique purposes, we should be celebrating our differences. In fact, how can there even be a "normal" when everyone is individual?

Do you know the worst time of my life was when I tried to be normal? I just couldn't get it right. My personality kept peeking through the costume I was trying to wear. I am not made for fitting in a box or a mold. God gave me too many dimensions to be uniform. He gave me a mission to be more, to have a rich, full life that does not involve me being like everyone else and doing what everyone else does.

I bet the same is true for you, though you might be afraid to accept it. What we need to realize is that hiding behind the label of "normal" doesn't change your differences; it only makes it harder to live in your own skin.

Enjoy and embrace the fact that you are unique. After all, God took great pains—seeing to every little detail—in the way He made you. Don't dismiss His craftsmanship. Don't discredit His choices. Be fully NOT-normal. Be uniquely you. BE MORE.

World changers are always on the path everyone else said wouldn't work! Don't be distracted by what others are doing. Keep going!
#BEMORE

SECRET # 65
SOMETIMES THE BEST THING YOU CAN DO FOR OTHERS IS STOP HELPING

We were made to care for one another. Our greatest traits as humans are our compassionate hearts and willingness to help.

But sometimes help becomes enabling. Sometimes assistance becomes codependence. When the lines are blurred and boundaries fall away, we can get trapped in behavior that stops being helpful and becomes a hindrance to the other person's growth.

If you find yourself doing more for the other person than they are doing for themselves, you are not helping. If the issues you are trying to help them resolve keep coming up or get worse, you are not helping. In fact, when they don't face the accountability of taking responsibility for their own lives or correcting behavior that is harmful, there is no incentive to fix what is working because you make it work. You are enabling them to continue with their bad choices.

There are times when we try to pull someone out of a bad situation and they aren't ready to change. In these cases, it is best to step back and love them from a distance. Pray for them. Let them know you care and will be there when they are ready to make an effort on their own behalf, and then let go.

It is hard to accept that we can't fix someone we love. We want to believe we can make a difference. What we don't realize is that sometimes the best help you can give someone is to let them figure it out on their own. Let them reach the place of brokenness where it's just them and God because this is where He can really do His work.

God is the great healer anyway, so get out of the mix until He says He can use you.

Having a caring heart and wanting to help is great, but sometimes we have to step away so those we love and want to help can be independent and healthy. Sometimes it takes being on your own to BE MORE.

Be careful not to get entangled in other people's problems if they have no desire to get free. That's called codependence, not help.
#BEMORE

DON'T BE AFRAID TO
CHALLENGE THE STATUS
QUO. DO THINGS
DIFFERENTLY. BE A
REVOLUTIONARY.

BE MORE . . .

MINDFUL OF YOUR
WORLD

QUIT LIVING AS IF YOUR PURPOSE IS JUST TO ARRIVE SAFELY AT DEATH. BE MORE.

BE MORE . . .
MINDFUL OF YOUR WORLD

Once we thought the world was flat and we could fall off the edge of it. Now we live in a global community where what we do in America has a great impact on the lives of a small tribe in Africa and the choices of the Chinese can change the way a town in South America functions.

We are no longer isolated by distance or lack of aware-ness. This huge world is getting smaller by the day as technology allows us to connect with people thousands of miles away as if they are sitting in a boardroom right next to us. Because of these far-reaching effects, it is time to really embrace the saying "Think globally, act locally."

The secrets in this section will show you how you have an impact on the entire world, even in the tiny section of the planet you occupy. You will understand how you can change the world through your actions. It is important to see that the work God has called you to do has a ripple effect and can reach all the way across the globe.

We started this journey with a small circle that centered on God. We took a step outward to discover ourselves, then reached further beyond ourselves into our relationships and our communities. Now we are discovering the world and the part we play in making it better. The ultimate goal of being more is recognizing the impact we have on the world from where we are and stepping into our greatness so the world is a safe and healthy place to be.

I pray you will be courageous to change injustices you

see, spread hope to those in need, and bring love—the love of God—to the far reaches of our world.